Bruce,
Ho at 1979
BRR

Halfway Up the Mountain

Halfway Up the Mountain

DAVID C. MORLEY, M.D.

Fleming H. Revell Company
Old Tappan, New Jersey

Unless otherwise identified, Scripture quotations are based on the King James Version of the Bible.

Scripture quotations identified PHILLIPS are from THE NEW TESTAMENT IN MODERN ENGLISH (Revised Edition), translated by J. B. Phillips. © J. B. Phillips 1958, 1960, 1972. Used by permission of Macmillan Publishing Co., Inc.

Library of Congress Cataloging in Publication Data

Morley, David C
    Halfway up the mountain.

    1. Middle age—Religious life.   I. Title.
BV4579.5.M67   248'.84   79-14734
ISBN 0-8007-1060-6

TO Marion, my wife, and our
children, whose love and
understanding have made my
journey up the mountain
of life a joyful one

Contents

Introduction

In the process of normal human development, middle age is a stage that all of us pass through. It's a time frame that has vague boundaries, but subjectively, it is that time of life when man begins to be aware of his finitude. Limbs that used to work with such effortless precision in our twenties begin to develop strange functional kinks. Pain begins to develop in areas that were free of discomfort, regardless of the physical stress. Wounds heal more slowly, muscle sprains incapacitate for longer periods of time. Shortness of breath may develop. Our bodies may begin to display the unsightly distortions of obesity from indiscriminate eating and drinking.

To all of us earth creatures with a definite span of life, these are uneasy developments. They remind us that, if life is a three-act play, then we are entering that last act. Then we must face the curtain. If life is an experience that is only related to this earth, these signs of degeneration and ultimate disillusion are very frightening indeed. When someone asked David Susskind, a man who spends his life asking other people questions, what he thought would happen when he died, he said in all honesty, "I believe when I die I will make the leap into the abyss. I would hope that my life on earth has accomplished something. If nothing else, through giving life to my children. The afterlife is oblivion. It's really quite desperate, tragic and frustrating."

Gail Sheehy, in her book *Passages*, suggests that one should meet mid-life with the vigorous renewal of life, be-

9

come involved with changes and new life outlooks, perhaps a new venture into narcissism. This formula sounds less ominous than Susskind's grim pronouncement, but gives little hope to frightened human beings increasingly aware of their own vulnerability.

To me, middle age is not the time when we should buckle up our belts, roll up our sleeves, and take another shot at youth. It's a time that cries out to man to consider his ultimate destiny, to think about the question of whether his life has significance only in terms of his earthly experience. Or possibly it is a time to dare to believe that life—that brief journey (of no longer duration than the grass of the field, as the Psalmist tells us)—may be an infinitesimal part of a longer experience that exists beyond this present life, instead of seeing death as the gateway to an enigmatic abyss. Perhaps it's the advent of a new kind of life that exceeds in beauty the most extravagant imagination of our earthly minds.

For a Christian, mid-life is a time when spiritual maturity can develop in its richest form, when the Person of Christ becomes a reality, the basis for a new and more meaningful relation with Him, which allows us to include Him in every innuendo of our lives. It's the time of life when the Christian, in ways that seem paradoxical to the world, becomes stronger, because he is increasingly aware of the strength of his Lord. It is a time when the fruits of the Spirit begin to flourish with the ripeness that is even evident to those who are not Christian. It's a time when the Christian can feel a freedom from the superficial stimuli that entrap the minds of most men—the greed, the egocentricity, the lust, the self-deception, and the denial of many men lose their attractiveness.

Christians do not escape the cruel process of mid-life, but should be able to deal with this phase of their existence with a greater sense of challenge than people who are not Christians. It is the peace, joy, and inner quietness that a Christian has available to him in the storms of mid-life that spark a more poignant message than the tongues of a thousand silver-tongued orators.

Mid-life, to a person whose perspectives are eternal, is a unique and exciting challenge, an exercising of his faith. To this kind of person, mid-life provides an opportunity for spiritual growth not before attainable. It is a time of fruition.

To those whose life is a spiritual vacuum, mid-life becomes an awesome shadow that chases away the dreams of youth and dashes the visions of the future. It imposes a legion of fears upon the beleaguered person. It may drive him into furious activity, like the frenetic dance of a marionette, but with each step of that dance lanced with a dread of what might emerge from the lengthening shadows that seem to be closing in upon him from all sides.

These are some of the things that we talk about in this book.

Halfway Up the Mountain

1
Emergence Into Middle Life

Middle life creeps in quietly, like a thief in the night. You may even hear its muffled step, that slight transgression, from sounds that a thief might make, but you ignore it. You know, for example, that the twinge of pain you feel in your left hip is simply a muscle strain that will quickly disappear if you stop playing golf for a few weeks, but you know that you cannot even think of doing that, since your handicap is fast approaching ten and you are hitting the ball farther than when you were in your twenties. So you bite the bullet and forget the thief as best you can, but the thief becomes bolder, and he makes his presence more clearly known. The pain becomes more persistent and even more intense. After a winter of almost total physical inactivity, the pain is there, bigger and more excruciating than ever. You are a very patient person and so you wait another year or so.

Then one day, when your guard is down, you do what you have been telling yourself to do for ages. Under the coercion of several members of your family, you consult your friendly orthopedic surgeon. You go to the hospital and he does his examination, which consists of a few flexion and extension movements. He then takes the inevitable X-rays. He will call you when he has read the wet prints. You walk out of the hospital quite confident

15

that you passed the test with flying colors. So you go home to wait for the telephone call that will confirm your diagnostic opinion of several years; that is, that there will be nothing of any pathological consequence in the X-ray pictures at all and that the source of the pain will be some insignificant muscle or tendon strain that will work itself out in a few weeks. You will rest, with perhaps some sonic treatments thrown in for good measure.

When the phone finally rings, you try not to pick it up too quickly. You immediately sense that the sound of the voice on the other end of the phone is not exactly the tone that you had expected.

"The head of your femur looks more like a football than a baseball, the way it should look. It's just a matter of time before you're going to need the operation." Suddenly the phone feels as slippery as a newly landed bass, your tongue feels thick and clumsy, and you don't have very much to say. Your heart, for some inconceivable reason, begins to beat wildly against your rib cage, and the tone on the other end of the phone sounds like a voice from outer space. "Are you there?" it keeps asking, but nothing comes out of your mouth. Your mind is filled with all kinds of images of people limping through life with artificial appendages. Everything from a ball-and-socket joint to a peg leg. And you try to fit yourself somewhere into that pathetic kaleidoscope.

Finally your voice mumbles, "Yes," weakly trying to camouflage the fact that you know that the thief has already made entry into your life and is probably establishing beachheads for some new offensive against your beleaguered body.

Perhaps your entry into middle life is less traumatic than that. It begins when you notice that clusters of hair are collecting at the bottom of the wash basin after you washed your face and combed your hair in the morning. You guess that maybe somebody had a haircut recently and had not had time to wash away the cut hair. But when the phenomenon occurs for three weeks running—the hairs that appear in the basin are not short segments of recently cut hair but rather long fibers that give every evidence of having been on somebody's head for some time—you begin to suspect that maybe something is happening to *your* hair. What is happening is that, ever so stealthily, it is beginning to fall out. You look in the mirror for any evidence of that dreaded blight. There does not seem to be any overt manifestation of this feared development. What you do see is plenty of evidence that the hair is much grayer than it used to be, but what you cannot see is that elliptical bare spot at the back of your head where the roots simply are not holding anymore. It is a spot you will not notice till several months later, but what you can be very sure of is that a lot of other people have been seeing it for a long time.

Or maybe this flash of insight comes the night you go to the Palm Court of the Plaza Hotel for evening dessert. You look around the shadowy room and begin to drink in the splendor of that magnificent replica of an age of affluence long past. The music of the lone violinist, mingling with the voices of the elegant people who occupy the tables, makes it seem like a beautiful dream. Then the waiter, with that Parisian sweep of his hand, presents you with a menu of endless desserts. The parchment is brown and the printing is black, and, no matter which way you turn the paper, the print does not come into focus. You might just as well be looking at some form of Sanskrit. You hope they have chocolate ice cream on that menu somewhere, because your eyes simply fail to bring that print into focus. For the first time in your life, you realize that you need glasses. Maybe this accounts for your recent avoidance of any kind of reading matter. It is not because you are indifferent to the magazines and books that you have always enjoyed. It is simply a combination of not being able to see the print and a mind that refuses to admit that changes of degeneration are beginning to manifest themselves in your body. That good old 20/20 vision that stood you in such good stead in the Navy Air Corps simply is not there anymore. And so, finally, you are driven to get your first pair of half-glasses. There is no way you are going to wear full glasses until you have to.

There is little question that the physical changes that occur in middle age are not only related to the physical system, which is beginning to manifest clear-cut evidence of winding down, but to a life-style that catalyzes these degenerating changes. In many ways, you are spoiled by the tumultuous currents of youth. The physical activity associated with the freedom from responsibility other than that of schoolwork, and your often-neglected duties around the house, conditioned your mind and body to a way of life that is far removed from reality. You were not aware, at that time, that the powerful forces of energy that surged through your mind and body would begin to diminish. In the dreams of youth, everything seems possible, but as you move into middle life, you begin to find that the winds blow less briskly and you have to deal with life situations that were invisible at the time of your youthful dreams.

Physically then, you gravitate into a job that is sedentary in nature. To walk or run five miles a day in the perpetual activity of youth is nothing—something you did not even have to think about—but in middle life, you do not walk five miles in a month. You use your car to go to the office. Once there, your activities are generally confined to one room. The lunch hour becomes truncated in time because of the pressing need to get things done that simply cannot wait. If you do plan to take a walk every morning, it soon becomes impossible, because there is not enough time available.

Any physical activity at home has to wait until the weekend, for the simple reason that you feel too tired when you get home at night. Even the weekend time for exercise diminishes, because this is the time that you begin to use for social commitments not possible during the busy week. At a time in your life when physical exercise becomes an absolute necessity, you unconsciously place it in a category of something that can wait until more important things are accomplished. To this plague of inactivity, your body responds in ways that are clearly predictable, but perpetually denied. Gradually your waistline expands. You might recognize it, at first, as a pleasant roundness—a development that at first may be looked upon with mild amusement—but when that pleasing plumpness gives way to unsightly bulges, the process ceases to be funny. And so the thirty-two-inch waistline gives way to a thirty-four, and the thirty-four to a thirty-six, and it seems almost incredible that you could have gotten into a twenty-nine not so long ago. The realization of these changes comes into your life in various ways. Maybe you find that you are wearing your belt two notches larger than you ever did before. You may find that your belt begins to show two lines where the buckle creases the belt because of the need for more girth after a meal. In the good old days, there was only one crease, but now the tummy does not feel comfortable with the buckle on the old notch.

Or maybe you are at the beach and notice the washboard abdomens of the kids in their twenties. You really cannot help but notice the difference between their abdominal concavity and your convexity. You surreptitiously pull the tummy in, as they told you in the navy, but you do not recall it took that much effort over a sustained length of time. Maybe that was because at that time you didn't have as much stomach to hold in, or maybe what you had to hold in was more muscle and less fat. From then on, you begin to be very conscious of pulling your stomach in, but what really disturbs you is how many times you forget, only to catch yourself when you see someone staring at your pot in a less-than-complimentary way. It all comes back like a bad dream, and then, quite suddenly, you slip into the Charles Atlas pose again and hope not too many people saw you in that moment of digression. You resolve that when you get home, you will launch a ten-year plan of exercise designed to produce in your body a muscle tone that will never submit to the ravages of time. You find that if the ten-year plan survives ten days, you are lucky. It, too, falls into the quicksand of procrastination which is another characteristic of this bewildering time in man's life cycle.

And so we see man invaded by silent forces that seem bent upon changing the endless physical potential of his body into something of rather specific limitations. Man will have to deal with peaks and valleys in all the years of his life. What a tragedy it is for a person to believe that the first peak is the only valid one and from then on his life journey is dedicated to colorless, if not tragic, descent into nothingness. What he must see is that the towering peaks of youth are replaced by the contained, richer elevations of middle life that are more geared to reality and, therefore, prepare him for the final stages of man's life upon the earth, which we call old age. We might better call it the age of completeness, when man through his experience contains all of the stages of his existence.

Man does not always like the things that happen to him as he moves through the different phases of his life. The process of acceptance has always been a difficult one for him. What he does not always understand is that acceptance has nothing to do with resignation and defeat. Acceptance is the first and most important step in an honest and meaningful resolution of any problem involving reality.

Human beings become very proficient in the act of self-deception. It is a mechanism that begins early in life and reaches a significant level of proficiency in the middle years. The art of self-deception relies heavily upon an important mental defense mechanism called denial.

Denial is a mental sweeping of the dirt under the rug, but that metaphor does not capture the total meaning of the mechanism. There is a mystical element in denial. It is like the magical thinking of childhood, "If I don't think about an unpleasant problem, it will go away." We all know the folly of that kind of thinking, and so very often denial of a problem provides further inroads for it into our lives.

In a way, we could get away with denial when we were younger. Maybe it is the character of the things denied that made the difference. It was easy to deny most of the pain in your ankle, sprained in the football game, because you did not want the coach to see you limp and call you to the sidelines. The raging fires of competition and the restored forces of a healthy, young body cancelled the negative effects of denial. They transformed what could have been a major offense into a minor misdemeanor.

This transformation is not easily executed in middle age. The fires of metabolism are stoked less liberally. The symptoms that we could have denied quite easily in youth begin to send us signals that are more persistent and less likely to be washed over by the tides of a metabolism less vigorous. The pain in the chest of youth, which was a transient muscle strain incapacitating today but gone tomorrow, now becomes something that might pertain to things more serious. We cannot ignore pain in the chest or any other part of the body in middle life because this symptom might be an indication of a degenerative change that needs careful attention. One of the great tragedies of today is that when medical science has so much to offer people, they do not turn up at the doctor's door until the condition has deteriorated to an almost unmanageable state. The man, who could have been helped with a little digitalis and nitroglycerine and more careful attention to his diet and exercise, turns up at the emergency room of a hospital, not to discuss the history of his symptom and some further helpful facts related to heredity and environment, but to be administered to by a cardiac team, who will make an all-out effort to save his life.

If the man had respected his symptoms, he would have gone to the doctor and then received advice and medication that would have prolonged his life. It is a sad fact that the closure of a coronary blood vessel has to be the only event that can cause some men to change their tempo from the charged-up pace of youth to the more fluid, contained movements of middle age. Some people move through life with their foot slammed down hard on the accelerator. How much of life they miss. From your own experience you know that you can see more of the countryside driving through it at twenty miles an hour than you can when your hands are white knuckled on the wheel and the speedometer reads seventy.

Perhaps the most prevalent example of denial of physical change in middle life has to do with the simple accumulation of excess weight. As a man's metabolism begins to mellow and his physical activity diminishes, the food that he takes into his body has less opportunity to be burned off and more tendency to languish into the fat deposits of his body. It is a revolting development in most people who enjoy their food. What seems to be unfair is that their appetites remain the same as they did in the flower of their youth. In those halcyon days, a person could eat all his appetite desired and not gain an ounce. Now the winds have changed.

As is so often the case, people meet these challenges of middle life with denial. In a kind of cruel reversal to the advent of lowered metabolism, their appetites become even more ravenous. Perhaps it is the universal response to loss. Some of these people become very skillful in their ability to camouflage the deformities that are obesity, but they are never really successful. Their skillful art of camouflage does nothing to allay the forces of accretion that, at some point, become so ponderous that even their art can no longer modify the unsightly manifestation of their indiscretions.

What is even more remarkable is that the majority of these people, who have sold out to their uncontrolled appetites, make no effort whatsoever to conceal their obesity in even the slightest way. We see men with abdomens extended as though they were in the eighth month of pregnancy, rather happily displaying their paunches as trophies from a hunt. They adorn themselves in white T-shirts which tend to accentuate their bulging abdomens. They demonstrate a disturbing tendency to pat their tummies not infrequently as though an abdomen were a pet bear that had climbed up into their laps to hibernate.

If these thoughts seem extreme, I would invite you to go to the beach sometime and view this spectacle of humanity as it passes by. There you will see the whole spectrum of humanity in every conceivable physical form. Before you is the arresting sight of lean, young bodies moving freely about the beach in some form of physical activity. The young are proud of their bodies, not only because of the way they look, but also because of their agility and their endless potential to perform physical feats. Even more arresting, on that same beach, not too far away, is a species of humanity that resembles beached whales more than human beings. There is not much physical activity in their camp. Their well-greased bodies have spread out their wide horizons to embrace all of the sun they can get. Their bikinis are often as brief as the young gazelles' cavorting about the beach, not so far away. What is most puzzling to me is that these obese people do not seem to be aware of what they have done to their bodies, and, what is worse, they do not care. The fact that they, through carelessness or greed, have made something ugly out of God's unique creation is almost humanly unforgivable. If God has given man a mechanism of such amazing potential as the body, one would think that the least a person could do would be to take care of it.

There is something in all men that shies away from responsibility. This is a malignant proclivity that is captured in the words of the old German proverb that says, "We want the roasted pigeon to fly into our mouths." Man wants to eat in the same way that he breathes. He does not have to think about his pulmonary functions. Nobody gets obese from breathing. It does not involve choice. It seems that when the element of choice enters the picture, man has problems. Very often the choice is between something that pleases his feelings versus something that is more appealing to his intelligence.

If he knows that his metabolism is slowing down and his physical activity is following suit, then he must realize that the mass taken into his body is going to exceed the mass burned up. His body cannot do anything but put on weight. It is a simple mathematical formula that is undeniable. He also knows that the good taste of the food that he ingests is temporary, lasting only for seconds or, rarely, minutes. Everybody knows these simple truths, but how easily he ignores them when the waft of the cooking food comes into his nostrils.

Yes, he can deny the reality of these physical changes of middle life, but if he does, he robs himself of the special challenges and blessings of that period and, maybe, ends up the prisoner of his own instincts. He was not made to serve his instincts, rather the other way around. His instincts were given to him to make his experience richer in each phase of his journey up the mountain. There is no question that there is a greater awareness of these degenerative changes today and that people are being moved to do something about it. The natural-food industry is booming. People are beginning to assess more carefully the things that they eat and drink. The sides of our roads are full of grim-faced men and women, dressed in various attire, jogging uncharted miles to keep their bodies in shape. These are people who are meeting the challenge of middle age. People who want to feel the healthy tone in their bodies as long as they have them to use.

Christians should be leading the vanguard in this movement. The Bible makes it quite clear that our bodies are the temples of the Holy Spirit. Should these bodies be saggy and soft, masses of flabby tissues the only function of which is to deplete them of energy? Should they be the point of ridicule of the people of the world who have much less reason to take care of their bodies? Christians, therefore, should be the most discriminating people of all regarding the things that they take into their bodies. No one should point the finger of scorn at any Christian's body as a mark of indulgence and neglect. There are more important reasons than that why the Christian should be meeting the physical challenge of the middle years.

For those people who have no hope beyond the present existence, the concept of man's finitude is very threatening. They view the degenerative changes of life with fear. What comfort can there be in reconciling to oneself the fact that his excursion on this earth is a brief one and that it begins with the vitality of youth, suffers through the degeneration of the middle years and the immobility of old age, and ends in the extinction of death. Man confronts himself with the thought that each night of sleep is a little death preparing him for a more extended one at sometime in the future.

There does seem to be some symbolic connection between the two phenomena, but certainly none that would give any thinking person a sense of comfort. The philosophies or religions that tell us that we live on in the genetic stuff of those whom we generate, provide us little solace.

We have said that the world generally deals with these changes of middle life with denial, and some of the people deny the process altogether by continuing in the same habits that dominated their younger days. The result is a metamorphosis into a physical being of hideous design. The grotesqueness of the body is exceeded only by its vulnerability to disease processes that are directly related to the excesses that formed it.

Others deny the changes in middle life by regressing into behavior patterns reminiscent of long-lost youth. That is not too difficult to understand. The phase they are moving toward has nothing to offer them in terms of things they consider most important. They look at the infirmities of the aged and see nothing in that phase of life that would be in the least attractive. And then, of course, beyond that lies the dark oblivion of death. But we will talk more of these in later chapters.

To the Christian these middle-life changes have a different meaning. The change that is so threatening to the nonbeliever is an opportunity for the Christian to exercise his faith and to experience the process of true Christian maturity. The mature Christian is a person who can deal with change. He can accept all of the vicissitudes of life and not deny nor complain about them. He sees them all as the manifestation of God's love. If God loves me, then He is going to provide an experience that makes life richer and more in line with His will. To the Christians, "All things work together for good to them that love God . . ." (Romans 8:28). How often we hear that Scripture quoted. How little we see it applied to real-life experiences. What God is really saying is that we should comfort ourselves with the thought that what happens in our lives, victory or defeat, wealth or poverty, sickness or death, all are indications of God's love and His interest in the design of our lives. If He brings sickness to us, we should be joyful for the opportunity to turn to Him more completely. So often in the bloom of health, we forget to remember the God who has provided that health. When we are in a position of weakness, we are more likely to acknowledge His strength, we are more likely to ask His guidance every step of the way.

Mid-life to the Christian should be a time of harvest. By now his mind should be richly infused with God's Word. His thoughts should be filled with God's peace that passes understanding. He should meet all of the challenges of mid-life whether they be physical, spiritual, or emotional. His life should shine like a beacon in a world where people are consumed with fear of dying but do not know where to turn except to satisfy the desires of their own instincts and to cling more desperately to the time that is slipping through their fingers.

To the Christian the changes of mid-life confirm the fact that he is involved in a vicious cycle of sin and death, which heralds the end of his finite existence, but what is the end for the unbeliever is the beginning for the Christian. What the Christian looks forward to more than anything else is the meeting with his precious Lord—the Lord Jesus Christ. My silent invisible friend all of those years is Someone that I shall see face-to-face. "For now we see through a glass darkly, but then face to face . . ." (1 Corinthians 13:12).

With these thoughts in mind, the Christian should not fear the middle passage of his life. He should view this period as a time of enrichment. The flurry of youth is passed. His life begins to fall into step with reality. He sees that he can gain a measure of control. His tastes become more discriminating. He begins to enjoy the things that he has, rather than long for the things he cannot have. He begins to learn about patience and endurance. The need for immediate gratification has diminished because he has learned that sometime in life we have to wait and the time of waiting ought to provide knowledge that one could not get in any other way. He is not afraid to face the reality of his aches and pains. He faces the reality of their meaning and does something about it. He does not continue in the unchecked appetites of youth. He modifies his appetites to meet his needs. He sees that the needs diminish as the metabolism slows down. He accepts that as a fact of life and takes the position of responsibility by doing something about it. He begins to enjoy the security of control that he has in all areas of his life. No longer driven by every wind and doctrine and every impulse that comes his way, his course is straight and true, and the radiance of that life beams out to the world the message of inner peace. And that is worth more than volumes of words.

2
Man's Narcissistic Nature

You have heard Frank Sinatra sing it a hundred times in that velvety voice of his that carefully articulates each word as though he were shaping delicate gobbets of sound. The song is, of course, "I Did It My Way." When Frankie sings that song with such depths of feeling, you sense he is telling you something very precious, something very important coming from the very depths of his soul. What he seems to be saying is that even though he may have made many mistakes in his journey through life and fouled up some other people's lives along the way, the important thing is that he did it *his* way, and that is all that really counts.

The message is that the most important thing in life is not what a person does but rather that he does it his way, or as Frankie puts it, *my* way. That kind of song, with those kinds of lyrics, seems to be the theme song of modern man: "I couldn't care less about other people's feelings or other people's ways. Mine is the only one that counts and that is the song that I'm going to sing as I pass through life. I'm going to follow my urges. I'm looking out for number one because that's the only number that counts."

If you visit nightclubs in New York, you will see a thousand people who are all doing it *their* way. On the surface they seem to be happy. Their beautiful teeth sparkle like pearls in the subdued light of the discotheque. The conversation is brilliant, a little bit naughty, and highly seasoned with gossip and just a pinch of profanity. But beneath the sparkling exterior of the well-turned-out faces, striking good looks, clothes straight from the tailors at Bergdorf's and Brooks Brothers are sad, shallow little people doing it their way. Along the pathways of their lives are strewn the bodies and lives of those who dared in any way to impede their glorious goal of doing things their way. On the pathway of their glorious pursuit are faces of unhappy, bewildered children—confused, rejected, old before their times—wishing that someone would see their way. But instead they see the ones from whom they want so much to have love being drawn even more deeply into the morass of self-love.

It is perfectly understandable why people are susceptible to narcissism. The infant is completely narcissistic. Unacquainted with this world, he is, at first, unable to believe that there are other creatures inhabiting this strange globe upon which he finds himself. Oh, yes, there is Mother, but in those early days the infant is not even able to understand who she is or what she is. She is simply there, but now somebody out there, rather than somebody he is inside of. During the first few months, if not years, of his life, the child is absolutely helpless, demanding service upon his every whim. When he cries, one of those giant creatures who surround him, moves quickly to meet the crisis and thus restore the infant to the equilibrium that he momentarily lost. Of course, a modicum of this narcissism remains in man's psyche as long as he lives. In fact, we have all seen examples of older people who begin to show a return to the narcissism of infancy. We have come to think of this as second childhood, however unhealthy this return of childhood is.

The fact that there are residuals of childhood in all of our psyches is not necessarily a bad thing. In a very real sense, it is important that we learn to recognize them as objectively as possible, because, if left unheeded, they have a tendency to dominate the whole personality. In fact, people who are quite mature in some areas of their lives show a predilection to be quite immature in other areas. The contained, self-confident businessman, tall and strong in the skirmishes of corporate warfare, on the golf course can be almost immediately transformed into a seven-year-old-boy, completely out of control when, after a Nicklaus-like drive, he shanks a wedge out of bounds. The unexpected appearance of the child in the stream of adulthood is often so sudden that the child is already into the act before it is recognized. That is why we should become aware of this propensity and recognize those situations that herald childish drives.

To me it is rather pathetic, if not embarrassing, to see many adults under the sway of this uncontrolled child from their past. Perhaps the haunting strains of song after song give us some indication of why this is so. To be locked in that childlike type of behavior responsible only to oneself, has become almost heroic in these latter days. The middle-life man who leaves his job and his family and takes off hand-in-hand with a twenty-plus-year-old, tuned-in secretary is not a fool, but a folk hero. He is not copping out or contributing to the psychopathology and tragic consequences of the bewildered people he leaves behind, but he is a real champion because he has the courage to do it his way. Suffice it to say that narcissism, as we have been discussing it, is at the root of this heroic compulsion to do things our way.

Many people use the word *narcissism* without really understanding its origin. Narcissus was a figure in Greek mythology. He was a handsome youth, in fact the most handsome of all created males. He was so handsome that one of the leading goddesses fell in love with him. Unfortunately, Narcissus did not return the favor. He would rather be off chasing mountain lions than languishing through the amorous ministrations of the goddess. When it was quite clear that the younger man was not going to return her favors, she became angry, as some jilted maidens are wont to do, and fixed it so that Narcissus would never be able to love another human being. One bright, sunshiny day, when the

Greek youth was dry of mouth and tired after having chased a few lions up the mountain trail, he bent over a pool of clear water to quench his thirst. As he bent to drink of the crystal stream, he saw, staring back at him, the image of his own face. It was love at first sight. The youth, having fallen in love with himself, could never fall in love with another human being. The goddess had finished the job that she had set out to do.

There are many elements in our culture that would encourage doing things our way, that would make us feel almost guilty for not doing things our way. We follow these heady tunes like the children followed the pied piper of Hamelin, dancing along in the streets, whistling our own tunes, every step taking us closer to the seat of oblivion. Think of the awesomeness of a nation of narcissists, a nation of people who love only themselves, each person making his own rules, writing his own script.

The narcissist has no sensitivity to the needs of other people. He is too consumed with his own desires. In a nation of narcissists, the only useful people would be the people who could be useful to you. Self-sacrifice would be an indication for immediate and prolonged commitment to a psychiatric facility. One of the elements that encourages this kind of thinking in our society is the great emphasis on competition. There are not so many willing to put themselves on the line in a really competitive situation. Men have their heroes, their ego ideals, who do the work for them. For example, when their favorite baseball player puts one into the right-field bleachers at Yankee Stadium they get almost as much a kick out of it as he did. When their heroes win, they win with them, and when they lose and begin to show their humanness, their former fans want to throw them to the lions. They rush to defend their narcissistic dreams. On the other hand, their narcissism is so tender that they cannot risk integrity in a competitive situation themselves. They know the names and numbers of all the ball players, but do not have the skill to throw a ball from home plate to first base in a straight line if they had to.

In many ways, people in their middle years are most vulnerable to narcissism. By that time, most people who have assumed only a small portion of success and achievement in this world know what it means to do things in ways other than their own. The narcissist, unless unusually talented, was batted out of the ball game in the early innings.

To some people, even to those who have contained the fiery coals of narcissism through their twenties and thirties, to the extent that they were able to complete a college education and become effective in some corporate position, the melodies of narcissism may come wafting into the windows of the mind in mid-life. Maybe after all of those years of self-sacrifice and beating his head against the wall in a job that does not seem to be going anywhere a man looks around to find his life is going nowhere. By that time, it is perfectly clear that the ultranarcissistic dream of becoming chairman of the board is out, and all there is to look forward to is a subtle but firm kick upstairs, where he passes the time until retirement, with all of the frills of an executive position but with none of the power. Then he inconspicuously moves off to spend most of his days following the daily caprices of the stock market and, maybe, looking forward to that five-o'clock cocktail that soothes the sharp edges of reality.

The position is essentially defensive because, in many ways, he is all punched out because of the activity of the early rounds. In that defensive position, narcissism can move in more quickly and transform a thoughtful, dedicated person into what they used to call in the navy a *one-way Charlie*. In those moments of vulnerability, he sees that, in many ways, he has neglected himself for others, principally his family. With a new kind of "objectivity," he sees that they have not really appreciated his valiant efforts. He forgot the nifty little sports car that he always wanted because the bigger four-door models carried more people, allowing more kids to get in on the act.

Now, in the silent brooding of his thoughts, as he bumps along the rails on his way home on the five-o'clock commuter, he has a new vision. It is a vision that includes himself. One in which he is free to do all of the things that he has wanted to do for years, but could not because his style has been cramped by the ugly restraints of responsibility. The dream, of course, is a narcissistic one. His wife, family, and all of the other contaminants of his life have been sterilized by this fresh new breath of freedom. These are the dreams of a Walter Mitty, the colorless, little man who struggled for day-to-day existence, and became a legend in his own time. In his mind this man who can hardly afford the monthly payments for his Chevy four-door now speeds along the narrow streets of Monte Carlo, with a tall, sinuous blonde at his side, heading for the gambling tables where he is at home with the glamorous background of European royalty. This character, who in real life is buried in some obscure corner of a large office, doing mundane work that everyone else refuses to do now becomes the commander of a submarine that has been the terror of the North Sea. When he walks into a room of the Royal Yacht Club of London, everyone grows silent. Pipes come out of the mouths, eyes raise from the newspapers. People are universally subdued by the awesome nature of this mysterious marauder of the sea, who actually would not know how to put an oar in an oarlock without his wife's guidance. In the world of his fantasy, he is commander of the greatest underwater fleet of all time.

As the man plays with these thoughts, yes even encourages them, his thoughts get closer to action. Why not buy the sports car he has always dreamed of? So one day this man, who had not even bought a suit on his own for thirty years, goes into a showroom and buys a $15,000 Porsche. His wife almost goes into shock because there are still three kids to put through college and the mortgage is still not clear on the house. She thinks that he has gone bonkers. He feels he has done the greatest thing since he joined the Marines against his parents' wishes. The rush of narcissism is so great in his blood that he is willing to try anything.

One more peep out of her and he is out the door and this time he really means it. Suddenly the options are limitless and all of the time, like Frankie, softly and very close to a microphone, he is singing the new hymn of freedom, "I did it my way."

Little does this pioneer of a new way of life realize that focusing inward represents a regression of the most primitive kind. In the pilgrimage through the life cycle, we move from the infantile period of complete dependency to periods of not only greater self-sufficiency but also to attitudes that can free us from the internal narcissism, which insists that the world revolves about us. The greatest sign of maturity in the human being is not to be found in his standing before a mirror, focusing all of his attention upon himself, but rather, in that his action can be directed easily to other things and other people. God, in that wonderful provision, anatomically constructed us to see other people, yet how hard we work to invert the natural process.

It is the Christian, of course, who has access to a way of life that can free him of his compulsive narcissism. And the person who is born again is born into a world where the focus of his life is no longer on his own narcissistic ego but on the Person of the One who brought about this wonderful transition, the Lord Jesus Christ. Not only does the focal point of his world change, but he finds himself in a world that goes far beyond the perimeters of the physical world in which he now lives. For into his finite world comes an infinite dimension. It is because the Christian has the infinite dimension that he can transcend so many of the tyrannies that so easily involve people without that dimension. That is not to say that Christians are not going to have problems with that narcissistic element of their personalities like other human beings. So many Christians forget the fact that even though they are born again into a new world of eternal dimension, they still have a few more years to work out in this finite world. For as long as they are human they are going to have to deal with all of the problems that human beings have to contend with. Nowhere that I know of does the Bible state that man will reach perfection upon the earth.

God's Word admonishes us to watch in these latter days, and part of that vigilance is observing ourselves in the light of reality. We must not deny our narcissistic natures by actively suppressing them from our minds or becoming so aware of the egocentricity of other people that we overlook our own. We must see it as a substantial part of our nature and something that we must contend with every day of our lives. I am sure that Satan sees this as one of those special points of vulnerability in dealing with human beings.

The Apostle Paul makes this remarkable statement, "I die daily." (*See* 1 Corinthians 15:31.) What he means by that, of course, is that he dies to the narcissistic self daily. It is interesting that this death should be on a daily basis. This clearly indicates that the death blow Paul dealt his ego on Tuesday was not going to be adequate for what was going to happen to him on Wednesday. Because on Wednesday, that same lethal blow to ego must be dealt. The ego, like the Phoenix, rises out of the ashes of yesterday to become alive every new day. Now, to the person who rides along on the crest of scientific enlightenment, this talk must sound like drivel of the most fantastic kind. Taken out of context these words sound like a barbaric assault on all that we have learned in modern psychology, but the words may sound less outrageous if we clear up some popular problems of semantics.

Ego in every-day parlance is often equated with egotism. Freud, the man responsible for the use of the word in modern day psychiatry, had no intention that *ego* had any narcissistic meaning. He used it to refer to the integrative part of the mind that deals with the needs and the problems of internal and external environment. Every mentally healthy person must then have a healthy ego. People who have unhealthy egos are not handling the problems of reality in healthy ways. To further clarify this prob-

lem, I refer to the work of Doctor Harry Tiebout, who was one of
the real pioneers in the treatment of alcoholism. Doctor Tiebout
distinguished between a big EGO and a small ego. The small ego
was Freud's basic structural component of all minds. The large
EGO was narcissistic, much like the tyrant that stood on the
surface of the globe with hands upraised, demanding that everything be done his way. Doctor Tiebout saw the large EGO with all
of its infantile autocracy as the nuclear problem of people afflicted
with alcoholism.

The ego I am referring to as part of the narcissistic nature is the
EGO—paradoxically the one that never grew up, for if the EGO is
a sign of nothing else, it is a sign of immaturity. In the process of
maturing, man moves away from himself and toward other objects and people. At one time in our development, everything was
simply an extension of ourselves. Things had value only to the
extent that they could gratify self-actualization. It was only later,
after we had left the autonomy of the nursery, that we began to
appreciate the fact that there were other people and things in the
world out there who had a special autonomy of their own. Hopefully the things out there began to interest us as much as the
things in our own unique world. On the pathway towards maturity, there comes a point when one can let go of his own egocentricity and become part of something bigger than his own self-
gratifying interests. So a person at some time in his life may find
the world of aviation much more interesting than the primitive
world of self. So that person is willing to sacrifice his time,
money, and all of the self-indulgent pleasures that the EGO demands to learn the difficult art of flying an airplane and perhaps to
pursue a career in that area. There may be many things about the
rigid schedule and ambiguous management policies that he does
not agree with, but he learns to live with them because he finds
pleasure losing himself in something that is bigger than he is. In all
of this, he never loses his identity and may even go on to introduce into his profession some new operation or technical break-

through that enhances the world of aviation as well as the world in general.

The fact that this person may be mature in the pursuit of his career does not, of course, guarantee that he will be equally mature in other areas of his life. The person who can be very thoughtful and understanding of the other person at work may be the very opposite at home, as he stalks through the house like a tyrant, demanding that everything should be done his way and forgetting the ways and needs of those who are close to him.

God never meant for us to lose our identities. Each of us is an expression of His handiwork, His creative power. To that extent we are unique and special. But He does not want us to revere ourselves. Our reverence should be directed only to Him. God desires that we do things His way, but only because He wants what is best for us. That is why it is so important to know God's will in everything that we do.

As we move further up the mountain, our perceptions should sharpen. They move away from the starry-eyed impetuosity of youth to the realistically conditioned insight of middle age that reminds us that all that glitters is not gold. May our sight never sharpen to the point where we do not need the wisdom and insights that only God can give! "The best-laid plans of mice and men" often go astray. The finite creature has limitations that he must learn to live with. One of the distinct advantages of the Christian life is that the Christian has access to a Power that transcends his finite nature. It is important to know that that Power is there, but it is more important to keep those lines of communication open. As Christians, we must never forget that we have our feet in two worlds. The art of Christian living is to be aware of that fact and not to lose our footing in either one of them.

I know that part of the meaning of Sinatra's song is that we should choose a way of life that is different from the common herd. What he is saying, essentially, is that nobody pushed him into a prefabricated world, he did things in life that he chose. If that is part of the sentiment, then I think that Robert Frost put it more beautifully in his poem, "Two roads diverged in a wood, and I took the one less traveled by, and that has made all the difference." The concepts quoted in this poetry are quite different from the petulance of the foot-stamping child who passes through life wanting things done his way.

God has a plan for each one of us in this life. He did not simply wind us up like tops and turn us loose in this world to see what would happen to us. How important it is for each of us to know what His plan is for us. To do things *my way* is to sell out to an infantile narcissism that cannot perceive anything beyond the perimeters of the nursery. Are we to follow the petulant impulses of a force that never extends us beyond its own pleasure, or to follow the direction of God's Spirit, a force that leads us into paths that we may never have asked for but that brings to us a depth of blessing exceeding our greatest hopes.

The middle-age person, unable to feel the inevitability of his own finitude, has a major problem dealing with the forces of narcissism. He is the warrior standing thirsty before the Fountain of Youth. His mind is caught up in a dreadful dichotomy, with one component harshly directing him to face the realities of his own existence. From here on to the peak, the climb will be steeper. The warmth of the base of the mountain is replaced by a creeping invasion of cold. He is moving further and further away from the vibrant focus of youth that made him feel so secure in his humanness. Now the pace slackens. The rocks have little green upon them and here and there are patches of ice. His feet begin to slip. Time moves more slowly. The conditions all demand change of pace—a new technique of climbing to deal with the change in conditions.

Another part of his mind longs for the pleasures of youth. He now has the experience and the knowledge that he did not have twenty years ago. His physiology may have changed, but his appetites remain the same. The pleasures he used to dream about are now available to him. He has, among other things, purchasing power. He can actually buy the car that could only have been a dream before. From this vantage point he sees that so much of his life was spent in providing for others. It is about time that he did things his way.

People whose philosophy only includes this world deal with this crisis with a mechanism they call renewal. This essentially involves a careful review of their lives with the intent of surgically removing any parts that interfere with the process of self-fulfillment or self-gratification. This surgery often involves wives, husbands, children, or responsible jobs, a clear separation from any process that interferes with the pursuit of narcissism. These surgical maneuvers allow the person to pursue the purest form of self-love. Devoid of such contaminants as responsibility and any form of self-denial, the person is now free to worship at the altar of his own EGO.

What a tragic little closet life becomes for such people! People pursuing their own image in the mirror of self-awareness are never able to be free of the primitive narcissism of their childhood. What a petty solution for the mystery of one's life!

What a contrast these hoarders of life are to the grandeur that awaits the person who can lose his life in the rich beauty of the Lord Jesus Christ! This person is not caught up in the insatiable compulsion of feeding his own ego. His ego is lost in the new perspective that he finds in the Lord Jesus Christ. As the years pass by, and as he grows in the knowledge of Christ, his identification with the Lord becomes more complete. With each day that passes, he gets closer and closer to his ultimate goal, which is complete identity with his Lord. The further he moves away from his youth, the closer he gets to the zenith of his ambition. The forces of spiritual maturity give him greater freedom from the compulsive urges of narcissism. In mid-life, he combines the dwindling strength of youth with the soaring power of spiritual maturity. He is not afraid to move up the mountain because the higher he climbs the closer he gets to that moment of direct physical and spiritual confrontation with the wonderful Person of his Lord. As the years pass by, he becomes less aware of the chilly winds of advancing physical age. He becomes more deeply aware of an inner fire that burns more intensely as the years go by. The strength and direction of his life are not based upon a mental renewal but upon the process of spiritual maturity that follows in the wake of rebirth.

The advent of his rebirth was the beginning of a mechanism, that enables him to reverse the forces of narcissism. He is now free to leave the cocoon of his own existence to become involved with a world that lies outside himself, to be in symphony with a life process that transcends the uneasy cacophony of this world, and to link himself with things of eternal significance. People who take advantage of this freedom become involved with a world that far surpasses the myopic perspectives of finite life. This person can be perfectly honest with himself. A new song comes from his lips—not a song of "my way, sung softly and close to a microphone," but a clear symphony of sound carried across the hills by the wind of a spirit that transcends the range of any radio wave. It is a sound that brings hope to all that hear it, first, in the heart of the singer himself, but also in the hearts of those that hear him; a song whose words bring peace to the heart of the singer; a song that says very simply, "I did it *His* way."

3
The Street of Broken Dreams

At some time in life, your feet touch bottom and you realize that the extravagant dreams of your youth are not going to be realized in quite the same way that you had envisioned. The oak-paneled office on the top floor of the gas building, with its beautiful view of the river, is never going to be yours. You are going to be a middle-management executive until your retirement age. This is a perspective that comes into focus in the life of many ambitious and talented men as they approach the middle years.

Some men react to it with bitterness. At first, one sees himself as a victim of an unjust favoritism—so-and-so got the job because he plays a better game of golf. One begins to suffer from an incipient paranoia. He begins to see all kinds of plots and counterplots designed to sabotage his position and well-being. He becomes the ploy in some monstrous plot that is bigger than he is. He gradually turns against the maternal-like organization that has been the basis of his security for so many years. He felt comfortable in its encircling embrace before, but now he begins to recoil as the embrace becomes strangulation. The organization's concern over every aspect of his life becomes a not-very-subtle device to monitor every move that he makes in order to undermine and, ultimately, get rid of him. This man's performance becomes mechanical. He now becomes a creature of survival rather than one whose life had a goal, a meaning. His driving ambition is now displaced by a consuming bitterness that makes every day of his life an interlude in hell.

For most people such as he, the paranoia never becomes psychopathic, in that they always have a hold on reality. So, although they may become cranky and irritable to their subordinates, they may even become craven to their superiors. They have been in the organization long enough to know that one cannot snap at the heels of one's superiors with any degree of success. When dealing with their superiors, they may be seething with anger underneath, but only show joy and sunshine on the surface. They hate each word of this deceitful dialogue, but they find themselves mouthing it with the thespian skill of a John Barrymore. Only brief gaps in their speech or transient expressions of blankness in their faces indicate that there is another process going on beneath the facade of compliance.

These people are under the continual stress of trying to be two different people at the same time. In psychiatry this dichotomy of opposing forces is called *ambivalence*. But the Apostle James identified this disrupting force many centuries before Freud included it in his lexicon, "A double minded man is unstable in all his ways" (James 1:8). The cancer of ambivalence relentlessly erodes the identity of every healthy mental tissue. So the instability, which began in the work situation, seeps into all areas of a person's life. The distrust he feels toward the organization is now directed toward his family. He may never have been the ideal husband or father before because it was quite clear that in the priorities of life business came first, but he was still civil to his family, as long as they did not bother him too much, and he was always a good provider. There were times when he seemed to enjoy his family, never for extended periods of time, but just long enough to give the family an infusion of ultimate importance, which is basic to the essence of any healthy family. In those days, the prime priority of business gave him an objectivity, if not a remoteness, that allowed him to make judgments in family affairs that otherwise he might not have been able to make.

Now his life is concerned with bitterness. The same deadly paranoia that dominates his life at the office begins to operate in the home situation as well, but in the home the bitterness is even deeper. He does not have to employ the same forces of control he does at the office. No one is going to throw him out of his position at home, so he becomes a snarling, brooding despot, unable to be sensitive to any of the needs of his family. He sees himself surrounded by thankless vampires who are sucking his life's blood. He becomes so wrapped up in his negative narcissism that the family feels that a monster is now living in the house. The wife gets a part-time job. The children become involved in a million activities—anything to get out of the chamber of horrors.

As the years go by, this blight of bitterness does not lose its intensity, but instead becomes more deadly, more pervasive. The wife looks with terror to that time when the children will leave home and she will be left all alone with the monster. These final years of life, that should be spent in peace, reaping the harvest of a long and productive life, will be spent locked up in a cell with a creature that becomes increasingly inaccessible and peculiar. The children seldom visit home. It is not worth it. The pall of gloom is too thick. Once home, they can hardly wait to escape to the fresh air of their own lives. The parents live out their lives in the wormwood and gall of bitterness. They pass from this earth in a cloud of despair, surrounded by a tiny circle of people who are bound by duty and the forces of their own guilt to pay respect to persons they never really knew. Subconsciously these people are glad that this bitter man no longer has to be even a small part of their lives.

There are other people in mid-life in whom the force of ambition has never burned with an intense heat. They dared, at one time in their lives, to be ambitious, but the dreams never reached

the extravagance of the would-be executives we have just discussed. They moved up the ladder of success to a respectable
level, not because of any driving ambition, but because they were
of adequate intellect and could take orders. When the fight to the
top of the pyramid became too vicious, they quietly stepped aside
and let the dogs fight it out. Any organization needs this kind of
men. They are the mortar that holds the bricks together. In a
sense they are like the eunuchs of old, they threaten nobody. You
can trust a psychological eunuch because you know that the dis-
ruptive forces of ambition lie like ashes at the bottom of his heart.
He becomes a faithful retainer, as reliable as the rug on the floor.

Needless to say, this person makes a colorless passage through
mid-life. The uneasy storms of paranoia never disturb the inner
placidity of his life. He adds little to the world he passes through.
When gone, he becomes a vague memory in the minds of those
who knew him. He pays his taxes and lives within his budget, but
in all of his life, he hardly makes a wave.

It is in middle age that the finiteness of man's life comes into
sharpest focus. No matter what our ambitions may have been, we
come to see their transitory quality. After years of striving for a
goal we may have held above everything else, we begin to see that
it, in itself, really was not that important after all. Beyond that,
we may even dare to take that perspective one step further—
maybe we as individuals, working out our own life scheme, are
not that important either. That is a conclusion that can lead to
utter despair or to freedom from the compulsory egocentricity of
infancy.

The response to this dimension of reality, which begins to show
itself most dramatically in the middle years, goes far beyond the
examples previously discussed, but the general trend is downward. Life becomes less exciting, for excitement is always something that happened in the past. Even the faces of the people we
see in ads are those of young people. No one would dare to
advertise the beauties of life halfway up the mountain. Life is

something that is young and vibrant; one is free of sore joints and dimming eyes. Most of us choose to ignore this changing quality of life—the fact that the clock is winding down. To allow this kind of perspective to come into focus in our minds would force us to look at some aspects of life that would disturb our mental tranquility.

All this talk of halting gaits and dimming vision is rather depressing. It sounds as though we were caught up in an awful process that leads us from the gloominess of broken dreams to the bitter immobility of old age and then mercifully to oblivion.

What do you tell a person caught up in such a dreadful cycle? You can tell him that he is not the only one caught up in this process; that things are not as bad as they seem if one just takes one day at a time; or you can be tough like the existentialist and say that life is what it is. You cannot change it, you have to roll with the punches. Do not concern yourself with yesterday or even tomorrow, today is where it is. Or you can point out to him that his job is not all that important. There are many other things in life that are much more important. To help someone who is in need is much more important than being executive vice-president of a big company that makes automobiles. To pay attention to his own children and to intelligently guide them through the storms of adolescence is much more noble than writing a best-seller on how to look out for number one. But how can you sell these ideas to a person whose whole life has been pointed to a goal that is now going to be definitely denied? That man's feet are on the bedrock of reality, but his heart is broken into a thousand pieces. It is little consolation to him that many other ships have struck that shoal. To him life has lost its significance.

He gets little consolation from the fact that visiting sick people in hospitals and taking responsibility for poor widows and children are much more important than the memos he expected to dictate from that oak-paneled office overlooking the river. I suppose the only thing that you can tell him is that the same things have happened to many other people. Why you know somebody, who was the executive vice-president of a big organization, who got the boot. Now he has a small store that sells bait to fishermen in the Thousand Islands. He has never been happier in his life. Each winter he spends three months in Fort Lauderdale. The man is happy to be out of the rat race.

The permutations and combinations of things that can happen in a middle-age period are endless. Just as infinite are the responses to these changes that vary from a fanatic involvement in health food and physical exercise to a quiet resignation that leads a man to his television set with the inevitable can of beer.

God did not design the different seasons of life out of some unresolved sadistic conflict. God's business, among other things, is communication. What He tries to communicate is that He is and that He has a definite plan for each one of our lives. God could fill all the billboards of the world with His propaganda. He could saturate the airwaves with His words and design a zillion miracles that would convince anyone that He is and that He is here, but that is not the way He does it. He gives man plenty of evidence of His handiwork, but he lets man weigh the evidence himself. God does not push His way into anyone's life; nevertheless, He never stops trying to communicate.

The specific message that He communicates in middle life is that life is now half-over. You have a lot to look back on and hopefully a lot more to look forward to. By now your life is taking some direction. You are on a specific task or tack. Your jib is no longer flopping in a temperamental breeze. You also begin to realize, with an emphasis you never felt before, that life is really a very brief voyage. You may even begin to wonder if it has any meaning beyond the endless need to survive. These are the kinds of questions that lead a man, for maybe the first time in his life, to give consideration to the ultimate meaning of his existence. Am I some inconsequential blob of protoplasm that was thrown into a pool of life to swim a few brief years and then shrivel up and die and never be heard of again? Without verbalizing it, this is what so many people seem to be saying. It is inconceivable to them that the God of the universe is just as interested in their grimy little existence as He is in the life of the man who sits in the White House. That is part of what the message of Christianity is all about.

It is the Christian who can deal most effectively with the impact of change in the stages of life. Firstly, the Christian believes that God has a specific plan for his life. He further believes that the plan He has for his life is one that God has already designed. It is also a plan that embodies not only the best for the person, but also for all of God's people. As Paul says in Romans 8:28, "All things work together for good to them that love God." This suggests that God has His hand in every turn of our lives. Therefore, what have we to fear? Now these are easy concepts to mouth, but to put them into working operation in our lives is something else again. It is hard at any moment of time to think that a disappointment or a tragedy can do anyone any good or can ever be part of a plan that God desires for that person's benefit. We, unfortunately—or fortunately—do not have eternal perspective. We see things from the point of view of a finite world. God, however, has the eternal blueprint. He can see beyond the brief events of our days.

It is by passing through the obstacles of middle life that we can gain the true maturity that Paul spoke of. In middle age, it is hoped the Christian is now quite familiar with God's Word. He has come to see it as the very blood of life that gives him sustenance for every day. He has seen experientially the power and efficacy of prayer. He has come to enjoy the incomparable fellowship of fellow Christians. Each day the Person of Christ becomes more real to him. He sees in his own life a more perfect identification with the Person of Christ.

Do I seem to be suggesting that Christians should be devoid of ambition, or that they should fall into convulsions of laughter after a defeat? If so, that is not my intention. I believe Christians

can be just as ambitious as other human beings. I don't believe
God had anything in mind that would lead us to believe that He
wants Christians to be an army of losers. God wants us to function at optimal levels no matter what we are doing. He gave each
of us special talents that he expects us to develop, but not specifi-
cally to put any one of us into the Hall of Fame. Expecting your
talents to carry you is all well and good, but, in your true heart as
a Christian, you must know that all of these things occurred not to
put you in a limelight. They occurred so that your life could be an
expression of what God can do in someone who turns his life over
to Him. The heart of the Christian should be a humble one. As
such, he can develop his talents to a greater degree than a person
whose god is himself or success itself. Defeats become learning experiences, not pits of despair. Victories become less ego-
trips and more the deep gratification that comes with a job well
done.

I am not suggesting that all Christians deal with the vicissitudes
of life in the manner that I have described. I am simply saying that
all Christians have the opportunity to deal with life in this manner. Tragically we see in the lives of Christians the same inconsistencies as in other human beings.

It is in middle life that we should begin to see the signs of
maturity in the lives of Christians. These are the fruits of the spirit
as Paul points out in Galatians 5:22, 23: "But the fruit of the Spirit
is love, joy, peace, longsuffering, gentleness, goodness, faith,
meekness, temperance. . . ." These, unfortunately, are not the
characteristics we see in many Christians' lives. What we see, too
often, is a person whose life seems to be the very contradiction of
what he claims it stands for. Instead of love, we see anger and,
instead of gentleness, we see intolerance. We see a harshness
which belies any sensitivity to the feelings of other people. What
we see, in fact, is the picture of a bigot whose whole life is riddled
with the forces of hypocrisy.

Instead of mid-life being a time of maturity and mellowing for

such a person, it becomes a time when he is less able to camouflage the inner forces of hate and bitterness. The signs of his
Christian immaturity break out like a rash that is visible to all.
These are the Christian complainers—the poor lot who look with
jaundiced eye upon fellow Christians whose lot in life seems to be
considerably better than theirs. These are the people who love to
wallow in gossip and enjoy the misfortunes of other people. These
are the people who are a blight on the face of the church, who
cause the people of the world to justifiably conclude, "If that's
what a Christian is, then I don't want any part of it."

When the world looks at the church, it should see something
quite different from the pictures that I have just described. It
should see a group of people whose lives are reflecting the words
that are coming out of their mouths. They should see a group of
people in middle life who are beginning to show a respectable skill
in whatever work they are involved in. They should see a group of
people who have a wide knowledge of what is going on in the
world. For so often Christian people are completely devoid of
knowledge of anything that occurs beyond the narrow circumfer-
ence of their own church or their places of business. I believe God
wants Christians to have something intelligent to say about the
things that are happening in the world today.

Christians should have a lot of intelligent things to say about
everything that is going on. We have a book, the Bible, that
exceeds the knowledge of any book ever written. When mid-life
looms, the Christian should be well-versed in the wisdom of
God's Word. Unfortunately, this is not always the case. Too
often he has a tendency to sit back and let others search the
Scriptures for him. This is not to say that Bible teachers are not
needed. God has given some of these men remarkable gifts of
insight, but the real teacher of God's Word is the Holy Spirit. The
Holy Spirit works with the individual, often pointing out, for that
particular person, an insight that is directly related to his life.

The mid-life Christian, then, should not only be a person who is well-versed in the general commentaries on the Word, but should have some special insights himself. He should not be just a student of the Word, the Word should reflect itself in his life. Faith without works is dead, says James. (*See* James 2:17.) What a sad spectacle to see a man or woman who mouths insights, but whose life is full of inconsistencies that seem to be devoid of any knowledge of the Word whatsoever.

In mid-life one should begin to have an understanding of his own personality. Through the turmoil of childhood, adolescence, and young adulthood, we had plenty of opportunities to see ourselves in a multiplicity of human circumstances. Out of the observation of these experiences should evolve a self-knowledge that is accurate. We should know our strengths as well as our weaknesses. What a sad spectacle is a person whose knowledge of himself is all bad or all good. God allowed us to go through past experiences to get an honest assessment of ourselves. This kind of knowledge should not be static. If we have weaknesses, we should strive for strength. If, however, the weakness is associated with a certain circumstance, we should avoid the circumstance that produces it. Paul put it this way, "Flee also youthful lusts . . ." (2 Timothy 2:22). If, for example, I know that I have a weakness for chocolate cakes, I should not hang around a bakery. Part of self-knowledge is knowing the circumstances that make one vulnerable. Many a Christian has fallen by the wayside because he has not forsaken the circumstances that make him vulnerable. There is no doubt that God can give us victory over personal weaknesses, but a Christian to whom God has given victory over an alcoholic problem, should not hang around bars to test the durability of his victory.

There are Christians who, in middle life, become very comfortable about their lives and, incidentally, their Christianity. They are essentially well-heeled people who have gained a certain status in business. They drive Lincolns or Cadillacs. Their homes are neat and very well equipped with all of the devices that bring comfort in modern days. Their children are well behaved, that is, they make excellent grades in school and keep their rooms neat and clean. There may be rumbles of ruthlessness in business matters, but usually they are vague, ill defined—the sour notes of a group of malcontents who can always see something wrong with everybody. Generally, the image of these people is good in the eyes of the world and of the church itself. They are rich, well traveled, have considerable business clout and are considered all-around good people.

They, too, are busy in certain activities. They often become elders. They are very active in their judiciary function. Many times they are fine speakers, rich in their exposition of the Bible with words that are exciting and moving. Even their prayers are sanguine with rich declarations of love for the Person of Christ. But very often in their personal life are flaws that are puzzling, if not sickening to behold. It would almost seem that at certain points the sensitivity of Christ in their life is blotted out. Great declarations of love from the pulpit are counterpointed by acts of grave insensitivity in their dealings with people of less stature than our Saviour. Harsh, unfeeling remarks of discrimination come out of their lips—out of lips that just a short time before were filled with praise for the matchless love of Christ.

To me the most important aspect of the love of Christ in interpersonal relationships is that it is infectious. The love I see in the Lord fills me with a love that beams out to other people. If the Christian does not reflect, in his behavior, the love of Christ, then I am wary about his relationship with the Lord. The people described above are manifesting a gross form of immaturity that makes Christianity seem like a cheap charade to a nonbelieving world.

This group of people think that Christians should never have any problems. In fact, if one is living a real Christian life, he will only know wealth, success, and a life of material abundance. However, if *they* fail, it is never their fault—they are betrayed by other people, often Christians in whom they have put their trust.

These people strive to grow old gracefully. By that they mean to retreat to a Christian community in some warm climate, where, surrounded by wealth and all.of the things that make them materially comfortable, they await a Cadillac limousine from heaven to carry them through the pearly gates.

I am not aware that God ever desired His children to grow old with this kind of gracefulness. As we pass through the middle years and beyond, our hearts and minds should be filled with a greater awareness of Christ in every aspect of our lives. For as each day passes, we grow closer and closer to that encounter with our Saviour, with the promised expectation that when we see Him, we shall be like Him.

To the Christian, middle life should be a special challenge, for he has all of the equipment needed to successfully handle it. He can view this winding down of his physical processes with an objectivity not possible for people of no faith. For the latter it is the beginning of the end—the harsh reminder that man's stay upon the planet Earth is but a brief one—and so he had better get all he can while he can. This involves a compulsive clutching at youth, not realizing that middle and even old age have treasures not to be realized in the turbulent phases of youth. So we see the grotesque, if not pathetic, picture of the middle-aged man and woman dressing and behaving as if they were in their twenties. It is easy to criticize these people, but this life is all they have and you cannot blame them for grasping at even tiny sparks of life. On the other hand, the Christian is not depending on this life as the be-all and end-all of his existence.

The Christian can laugh where other people cry. The Christian can feel joy when the hearts of other people are filled with despair. Because of who he is, the Christian can have victory where others can only taste defeat.

The street of broken dreams holds no fear for Christians. The integrity of a Christian's life does not depend upon the fulfillment of some youthful dream. The Christian will have his dreams, as all men need dreams, for as Solomon said in his infinite wisdom, in Proverbs 29:18, "Where there is no vision, the people perish. . . ." And so, the Christian will have his earthly dreams and many times these dreams will be broken, but above all and beneath all is the pervading vision of all Christians—that is the day when they shall see their Saviour face-to-face. Earthly dreams will be forgotten then, for everything will be in proper perspective. They will not regret the dreams, nor will they regret that many of them were never fulfilled. Perhaps they will see that so many of them were ego-trips, the innocent dreams of children in a never-never land.

4
The Role of Victim

"All the world's a stage," Shakespeare once said. And the people who strut and fret "their brief hour upon that stage" have many roles from which to choose. But the role most popular in all ages, and maybe even more so in middle age, is that of the victim.

One of the most important reasons for this is that in middle age we begin to experience some real-life disappointments and defeats. As we mentioned before, the tender dreams of youth begin to whither in the strong rays of reality. For example, I may have to live with the fact that I am never going to be a vice-president. I am going to be a salesman all of my life even though down deep in my heart I never really stopped believing that that dream could be true. If I had been sent to Detroit instead of Toledo, I would be sitting in the front office right now. The fact is I was sent to Toledo. There was nothing that I could do about that. It was a corporate decision beyond my control. I was the victim of forces over which I had no jurisdiction.

No one can deny that we live in a world where we have to deal with many forces over which we have no direct control. There is nothing much we can do about the weather, for example. We have not yet developed, to any degree of sophistication, the technical expertise to make it rain or make the sun shine when we want to. We can complain about the rain or we can come in out of the rain and do the things that we have been putting off until that rainy day, but we cannot turn it off or on as if it were coming out of a spigot in the kitchen.

When driving along the highway, we cannot do very much about the behavior of the other drivers on the road. All we can do is deal with the problems of driving our own vehicles. There is an endless array of examples to illustrate the fact that in many of life's circumstances the role of victim is a viable one.

We can always find a reason, over which we have no control, for not doing what we know we should do. This predilection to be the victim is something that starts early in man's life. It is part of a vast network of self-deception of which we should be aware.

The child learns very early in life that the victim has certain rewards. How many times have you witnessed a child's quarrel where one of the combatants quickly turns to his mother with the statement, "He hit me first"? What the child is saying, in effect, is that it is not his fault that they are fighting. It was his brother or sister who hit him first. He knows that if he can convince his mother of this, he will be cuddled and soothed, whereas, his monster brother will be punished immediately or when Father gets home. We can see the subtle appeal of this role of the injured one that we all have tucked away in our psychological armamentarium.

As the injured innocent continues through life, he refines that role. He can readily explain any of his deficiencies on the basis of cruel forces over which he has no control. The reason that he flunks geometry has nothing to do with the fact that he did not bother to learn the theories or the theorems. It had everything to do with the probability that the teacher does not like him.

The reason that he did not make the starting position at quarterback on the football team was due to the fact that the coach saw him drop three punts in a row in scrimmage and that awful image never left the coach's mind. It may have been a lot more related to the fact that he gave up on himself that fateful afternoon and destroyed his chances of ever making the varsity squad. If he had done a little more research, he may have learned that the great players in any sport are often people who have bounced back from situations much worse than the one that seemed so horrendous to him, and by practice, determination, and a real sense of humility have become the real superstars in their field. There is something about human nature that makes it mobilize all of its positive forces from a nucleus of humility. The victim, of course, can never reach that point, for in reality, humility breeds responsibility and a willingness to do the job without any outlet of excuse. The victim, on the other hand, can never assume a position of responsibility. His whole life becomes an endless chain of rationalizations and excuses. Behind the veneer of a dialogue that is humble, lurks the ugly head of arrogancy. His message is essentially this, "I am basically perfect, for if this obstacle or that one is taken away, the flow of my natural talents will make me superior in everything that I do. If I were not victimized, I would always succeed." By assuming the role of victim, he avoids the awesome process of responsibility.

We must realize that in our society there is a tremendous pressure to succeed and the whole concept of self-acceptance is intermingled with achievement. The principle that perpetuates in the world is that the worth of the human being is directly proportionate to his ability to be successful. The world is very tolerant with the successful performer. It smiles indulgently at certain outrageous aspects of his behavior, thinking it part of the spectrum of his charisma. In fact, the world rather prefers its heroes to be somewhat naughty. The message is that one does not have to be "good" to be "good." It's a subtle put-down of the power of God. What people do not realize is that it points out a characteristic of God that is totally inconceivable, based upon human experience. God gives human beings talents with no strings attached. It is not for us to know why He gives some people certain talents and other people quite different ones, but this we do know, if God gives a person a talent, He never takes it back. The only thing that can destroy that talent is the person himself. If God gives someone a talent for painting, God does not rescind that talent because the person ignores the One who gave him that talent, or even if he uses that talent for things that are contrary to God's law. Some of the most talented people in the world are people who have completely ignored God or speak of Him in less than complimentary terms. If anything in human experience confirms the fairness of God in relationship to His creatures, it is the fact that once He gives a person a talent He never takes it away from him because of bad behavior. Each person has the chance to either develop or neglect the gift that God had given to him with no strings attached.

It is interesting that so many people blame God for the bad conditions that prevail on the earth. "If there's a God, why does this tragedy occur?" they ask. Or, "Why did that innocent child die?" God allows these things to happen because He has given man a free will. That freedom has no qualifications as far as God is concerned.

There are people who become very proficient in the role of victim. The whole life as an individual becomes a tragedy. The poor victim struggles against forces that are too much for him. The game, which started in childhood as an attention-getting device, has evolved into a permanent life-style.

Some people have built their role of victim around a nucleus of physical ailments. One saw early in life the effectiveness of sickness as a way of manipulating life's circumstances and especially as a very good device for getting other people to do things for him. He had not prepared for the exam, so he suddenly developed a stomachache that confined him to his bed. People are generally sympathetic to those who are sick. The person, whose major problem is that he is unprepared, not only gets the pleasure of languishing in bed but also gets the undivided attention of a doting mother whose maternal instincts are fired off like a rocket because one of her chicks has been wounded. The chick, who may not be as wounded as Mother thinks, plays his role to the hilt even though there may be occasional paroxysms of guilt because he knows that he is overplaying his part.

This charade, which all of us have indulged in at some time in our lives, is not so pernicious when it is a single or infrequent event. What is dangerous is that it presents to the human mind a viable way to handle any unpleasant situation in life. It also introduces him to the heady experience of manipulating other human beings for his own convenience.

We all know people who began as sickly children standing on the sidelines watching the world go by. If we observed them closely, we could see that they were lonely people, often quiet and withdrawn. As children we tried to get them into our games. Our enthusiasm was high and our patience was low. Our natural impulse to join and compete overcame our other delicate impulses of empathy that would have made us continue to coax these reluctant dragons to enter the fray. And so we left them to their silence and their loneliness and their rage. Yes, rage, because beneath the surface of that pale little face dwelt a basilisk of anger that slowly began to permeate every atom of that mind and body.

"For as he thinketh in his heart, so is he . . ." said Solomon in Proverbs 23:7. The truth of that proverb will be reiterated several times in the pages of this book. Nowhere is this axiom confirmed more convincingly than in the lives of the people who dedicate their existence to the role of victim. A victim can never win. The losses in his life, which are endless, are always due to the failure of other people or events beyond his control. The unspoken word is, then, that if he had not been victimized, he would surely have succeeded. By this mental ploy he can always protect his invincibility. If he runs a race with weights attached to his legs, he will lose, but the hidden inference is that if he had no weights, he would surely have won.

People who allow themselves to fall into this mental pitfall are victims of a false sense of justice and dedicate a great deal of their lives to collecting injustices. Their problems in school are due to the incompetency of their teachers. Their less-than-meteoric rise in the echelons of the corporation are due to the unfair caprices of those executives higher up on the ladder who open doors for their friends but do everything in their power to impede the progress of these innocent victims.

The role of victim is no better exemplified than it is in the middle-aged housewife. She may have acquired the role of victim early in her life. In youth she could mask it with her physical attractiveness which may have more than compensated for a chronic whining that was known only to those very close to her. The earlier years of marriage were lived in a busyness that muted the chorus of complaints. Her objections were endless, but were lost in the activities of bearing and raising children. All through the years the hard core of the victim penetrated more deeply into the whole being. Very early in the game the husband learned to turn her off. Their conversations became monologues, with the victim never tiring of recounting the insatiable cruelty of an unrelenting fate.

In the early years the husband listened with some sympathy. His excursion into the land of child raising, which may have involved changing an occasional diaper or trying to soothe a teething infant, only made him glad that his duties carried him away from this center of confusion and frustration. As the years passed, his sympathy diminished. The children were growing older and therefore reaching the time when they would become more and more self-reliant. The ensuing years had made the time away from home more meaningful than the time with the family. This subtle shift of priorities was occurring through all of the years but manifested itself more boldly in the middle years. These were the years when the demands of the husband's work were growing greater. He was more valuable to the company because his years of experience were now making him an expert in the narrow vector of his special work. Also the field was beginning to spread in such a way that he had a good idea of his chances of making a showing in the race. The problems at home were far removed from his mind. They seemed relatively unimportant vis-a-vis the things that were going on at the office. His tolerance of the complaints of his wife began to abate.

Before long, it became quite clear to him that his wife blamed all of the problems at home upon his ever presence at the office. The sympathy that he felt for her in the early years began to subside. No longer could he understand the basis of her complaints. After all, did she not live in a $150,000 home, drive a Mercedes convertible, and possess endless credit cards? To him it made no sense.

To the woman, further developments of middle life are a heyday, because now she can enter into her role of victim with relish. The children are either grown up or gone. She has more time to think about herself. The menopausal crisis is upon her. Her husband shows less and less interest in her and her problems. His behavior is only confirming the fact that he is the monster she always thought he was.

As time passes, her role of victim expands the inner tide of self-pity which wells up within her to fill every nook and cranny of her mind. If she was cut off from the world before, now she sees herself completely abandoned, for even her friends begin to turn away. They have heard the litany of her complaints too often. They have no sympathy left for this creature who seems not to want to do anything about herself. Her whole conversation circles around her sad plight in life.

She meets the symptoms of middle life not with denial, but rather with the desperate clutch of someone needing reaffirmation for her way of life. She often becomes the bane of the medical community. Her symptoms are puzzling and often exceed the boundaries of medical knowledge. She bounces from one doctor to another like a ping-pong ball. Nowhere does she find satisfaction. More and more she encounters rejection. She has not only become the victim of a heartless husband and cruel metabolic forces, bent upon making her a cripple, but, above all, the victim of a medical community that will not even bend a sympathetic ear to her complaints.

We have all seen victims of this type in our experience. They are sad, isolated people whose life ends in the exile of their own self-pity. The life-patterns of the victims spread like a spider's web over every area of their lives. Each year the web spins its fibrils to further contours and finally immobilizes its victims.

The role of victim may be more subtly enacted than the examples just described. The majority of people in a society that holds competition and superiority of performance of supreme importance are ripe for the role of victim, because, although the role of victor is desired by all, it does not take us long to learn that only one person wins a race. He usually wins that race because of natural abilities and the willingness to work on improving his talent, far beyond the willingness of most people. So in a race of ten people, only one will win and nine will be losers. How these losers respond to that loss will determine their fate in future races in life. The person who learns from his loss will someday win races himself. The person who makes excuses for his loss—the victim—will fall into a pattern that will guarantee an endless string of losses in the future. His whole life will be dedicated to losing, and the dialogue of his life will be an endless dirge of why he failed to succeed.

Examples of this subtle self-deception are seen very often in the realm of the business world. The structure of corporate life lends itself easily to those who prefer the role of victim. The executive ladder of success is built in the form of a pyramid. The bottom rungs of the ladder are occupied by many young and eager candidates. They view the towering apex with admiration and confidence. They see it as the likely destination of their ascent in the business world. It does not take them long, however, to realize that as one climbs higher on the ladder, the rungs become narrower. More seeds fall by the wayside. The opportunities for the role of victim becomes greater and greater. From the grumbling masses of those who phase out, at some point early along the ascendency of the pyramid of success, we hear the groans of countless whining victims each describing in his own way the many reasons why he was stuck at some wider rung, near the base of the pyramid. Many of these victims see their destiny in terms of personal bias. The other man was chosen for the job because he married the boss's sister-in-law, or because he and the boss play golf at the same club. Still others blame it on the prejudice against the educational institution where they studied. If they had attended Yale instead of Podunk College, they would have ascended the corporate ladder with the sure strength of an eagle.

Perhaps the first few bumps can be met with an objectivity that becomes less accessible as the person encounters similar crises in the future. It is at middle age, when the person has encountered enough setbacks to realize that the climb up the ladder will be forever impeded, that there germinates within him a growing bitterness against all of the forces and people he feels victimized him. He has become inaccessible at work and at home. His effectiveness as an executive declines because of the brooding bitterness that gnaws away at his mind. Now he becomes a hard-core victim, a man bitter against life and all of the forces that operate in it. He becomes a human computer, finding his only solace in his ability to fit into the special niche in the system, but the zest has gone from his life. All his time is spent licking his wounds, cogitating on all of the ramifications of his victimized life.

There are, of course, other ways to deal with these shocks of middle life. Some people substitute new value systems for old. The old goal of climbing to the top of the corporate ladder is replaced by a new goal of raising the best orchids on the block.

The new goal is entirely different in character from the old. The competition is less threatening. Indeed, in the new field, there is comradery, a healthy elitism that is very much different from the bitter winds of paranoia that blow in the corporate scene.

The kinds of alternate goals are endless—from the desire to break ninety in golf to learning a foreign language. This kind of mental development is a very successful way of taking the sting out of the loser's role. The burning obsession of the victim loses its hurt like the boil that has been lanced. He, now, is able to live with his loss, for the thing lost is less important to him. Even so, beneath the surface of his mind still burns the coals of his discontent. He will be able to function better than the man who has never come to grips with his loss, but in many ways he is like the racehorse that has broken its leg and will never be able to run again. It is nice in the pasture with all of that delicious, green grass, but he looks with longing eyes across the fields to the racetrack where the thoroughbreds are training for the race.

Christians, of course, need never be losers. This is not because of some clever psychological maneuver involving the transposition of value systems or the employment of some altruistic cause. Paul says "In all these things we are more than conquerors through Him that loved us" (Romans 8:37). Christians may find themselves anywhere in the world system. They may be in the corporate hierarchy or involved in a profession that is independent of any system. The top priority of their lives is to know Christ and to reflect His love in their lives. If they are in the corporate system, they should recognize that the most important reason they are there is to glorify Christ. This does not mean that Christians must resign themselves to the broader rungs of the bottom of the ladder. They, too, can climb the corporate structure, but for a different reason. The man or woman without Christ climbs the ladder because of an inner compulsion to better himself. It is through this success that he gains identity. By succeeding he is able to accept himself. The Christian gains his identity through his identification with Christ.

So failures have a different meaning to the Christian. They are trials or tribulations that God has promised on the road to spiritual maturity. The role of victim has no place in the life of the Christian. It is completely meaningless in the life oriented around spiritual values. To the man of the world, a burnout at the base of the pyramid is tantamount to disaster and quick descent to the role of victim. To the Christian it is a learning experience or an opportunity to demonstrate to the world that he has something within him, a substantial something that can transcend any defeat. It is not an illusion of "pie in the sky by and by," but a strong, indwelling power that can overcome anything that the world can dish out.

This does not mean that Christians are immune to the role of victim. They are human beings like all of the other members of the human race. Maybe before they became Christians they were more deeply involved with the pernicious role. When a person becomes a Christian, he does not immediately shed all of the defenses that dominated his life before he became a Christian. When a person becomes a Christian, he is able to look at himself with an objectivity impossible before the Holy Spirit added a new dimension to his life. Contemplation of the hideous perspective of the victim within did not immediately cause the ghost to vanish. After all, it was this identity that helped that person to deal with all of the inexorable facets of fate before he became a Christian. One does not easily let go of the lifesaver if he believes that it has been keeping him afloat for years. It is only when the truth in Christ deepens and the reality of His existence becomes known that the person begins to surrender psychological props that kept him going so many years. Some people are never, ever able to let go the neurotic mechanisms that dominated their pre-Christian existence. As a result, all of their Christian experience is contaminated by this ugly blight. They are never able to let go the familiar security of a life perspective that sees them as victims. They cannot accept the fact that the Christian is a conqueror through his relationship with Jesus Christ. One can be sure that the ultimate person the Lord had in mind, when He created us, was not the brittle, uncertain person who clung to his role as victim before he had knowledge of the Lord. It is the miracle of Christian experience that God can take the pretzels of the life formed in the godless oven of the secular world and transform it into a thing of beauty and strength. This is the transformation that mystifies the world outside. This total change is so seldom seen. What a pity that God's power can so easily be strangled by a lack of faith.

One might object to these thoughts, pointing out that in the history of God's people there have been many souls who have died a martyr's death, the implication being that a martyr is a victim of the cruel forces of this world over which he had no control. Contrary to this thought, the martyr is the greatest victor of all, because he is willing to lay on the line the greatest thing that he possesses—namely his own life—to prove his love to an all-loving God.

You might further object that if God is a loving God, He would never see His loved ones suffer. He would summon a legion of angels to destroy the heartless assailants, but, again, God withdraws this prerogative. Indeed, He could summon a million angels to destroy those evil men, but God has given us a world that is characterized by free will. That is not to say that God does not interfere in human events. His request for us to pray and His insistence upon the power of prayer certainly indicate that He can modify the events in human experience, but, by and large, free will prevails. Christians sometimes experience disaster, but not because they are victims. If their lives are lived in the will of God, they cannot be anything but conquerors. Many times the tragedy of a Christian's sickness and even death can be the vehicle of turning many people to Christ. I cannot help thinking of a very courageous and lovely woman I knew in my own practice who, in early mid-life, was struck down by cancer. With the courage of a lion and the faith of a saint, she overcame her first encounter with this dreaded disease. She lived five more years—not altogether pleasant years from the human standpoint because she was under powerful medication—but, nevertheless, she continued in her tireless service for her Lord. Eventually she died, but the testimony of her vibrant faith and unwavering love for Christ lived on as a testimony of the kind of Christian maturity that had more impact upon the lives of other people than a thousand sermons. Not once in all of those years did she complain. Not once did I ever hear her lament the fact that she was struck down by this ravaging disease in the late springtime of her life. From the human point of view, this kind of experience makes no sense at all. It seems totally without reason. And yet God's logic, which transcends human understanding, was a stroke of brilliant logic because, in this case, it broke down the barriers of unbelieving people who could never have accepted God's logic from any other perspective.

When the Christian finds himself embracing the role of victim, he knows immediately that he is involved with a life-style that is inconsistent with his spiritual nature. He is inviting the old man to come in and take over the running of his life. It is the dog returning to its vomit and the washed sow to its wallowing in the mud. As long as we live, we will have to contend with forces that operate in a less-than-perfect human being. We can change the focus of our spiritual attention by a slight alteration. Peter did that when he was walking toward the Lord on the Sea of Galilee. The struggle never ceases, but God gives us the strength to surmount every temptation. With victory, we become stronger. It becomes easier to trust the Lord just a little bit more. The role of victim begins to fade in our memories. At some time, it reaches the inappropriateness of some of the habits of our younger days. We look at it like the long-forgotten teddy bear of our nursery days and toss it in the corner with all of the other stuffed animals. Today our business is with things that are alive.

5
Death—From Mid-Life's Perspective

At some time in mid-life, we begin to know more dead people than living ones. Even so, our minds tend to avoid any confrontation with this mysterious process. In medicine, we frequently are called upon to view bodies vacated by the forces of life. It is never a pleasant experience. One is often confused by, if not guilty of, the quick onset of his own objectivity in regard to that dead person, because the mass of motionless protoplasm that lies before him appears more like a wax effigy of something real than the real item itself. What is gone from the body is the dimension called life. It has no color or shape. It defies all of the measuring devices known to man. A mountain of it heaped upon the platform of the scale would not cause the needle of the scale to deflect in the slightest degree.

Pathologists have seen hundreds of bodies in all kinds of deadness, but not too many of their curiosities are peaked to wonder where that life process went. They are usually more interested in the weight of the liver, the microscopic picture of the cerebral arteries, or the degree of degeneration of the heart and kidneys. In physics there is a principle called "the law of the conservation of energy." The law, simply stated, is that energy is never lost, but merely changed from one form to another. What happens to the energy of life when something ceases to live? It is a question philosophers have grappled with for years, but the answers are speculative. Placed in the context of scientific logic it makes little sense at all. It is just something that happens. We all must pass through it someday. Meanwhile, on with the show.

In spite of years of evasion, the world is beginning to confront this mysterious, if not unpleasant, subject. Doctor Elisabeth Kubler-Ross has written a book called *Death and Dying* where she attempts to objectify the subject so that we can talk about it like yesterday's baseball game. It is thought that this kind of no-nonsense confrontation with the subject will take away some of death's sting or horror in the hearts of those people who must make this sometimes not-so-gentle transition into oblivion.

There are reports of people who have supposedly been medically dead, who, by some flaw in the process of transition, come back to dwell in the body they vacated just a short time ago. The tales are often different in content. It is only through a liberal exercise of imagination that we can bring these facts into any meaningful pattern. The process continues to draw its cloak of mystery about itself. Men are now brave enough to talk about the phenomenon of death even with those who are actively involved in the process of dying itself. As a result, the victim seems less awed by the process through the simple mechanism of being able to talk about it. I am not so sure that his being able to talk about the subject gives him any more real understanding, but talking about it is better than avoiding the subject altogether, as though it were something that did not exist.

In our younger days, death was there, but usually something that happened to a distant and aged relative, or like a bolt out of the blue to a schoolmate or acquaintance down the street. When the subject came up, it was quickly shooed away like a dog that had wandered on some freshly seeded grass. It was the kind of thing little children should not think about. It caused them to have bad dreams or made them into strange little children who stared at the other kids playing outside from behind the drawn curtains of their bedroom windows.

Death intrudes into our lives more forcefully when we move into the twenties. These are the times of horrendous automobile accidents, the wiping out of young lives in their prime by some sudden juxtaposition of error and neglect in a vehicle that was probably going faster than it was supposed to. Or, as has been too often the case in this century, the savagery of war brings the reality of death into focus with a sharpness that is searing to the mind. Certainly many people of my generation—World War II—had countless friends and acquaintances who never came back from the field of battle. Beautiful young people so full of life and the joy of living were forever silenced to this earth. They exist, now, as vague images in some distant compartment of our minds only to be recalled when some place or person brings them into focus again for a nostalgic moment, then off again to the anonymity of their hiding place in our minds. Yes, death can be brought into focus in a very emphatic way in those years of young adulthood, but in most cases, the subject finds little opportunity to root in minds that are actively involved with the stimulating business of living. The soil in the minds of those that are halfway up the mountain is better able to nurture the thought of this process than is any earlier phase of man's life. In the mid-life years, the thought becomes more tolerable. Not only is it something that can happen to somebody else, but more importantly it is something that can happen to the person himself.

Usually it is mid-life that a person is first led to make a will. If he were inclined to do so in his earlier years, he would be thought to be either excessively morbid or simply strange. Maybe one of the factors is that in mid-life man begins to accumulate some possessions that might be worth leaving to somebody else. The step of making a will is usually taken under the advice of a lawyer who is more acquainted with the practical effects of death upon the dependents who are left behind. What is a staggering statistical figure is the number of people who leave this world with no wills at all. Most of these people, until the time of their departure, could never really accept the fact that they were involved in a process that had a beginning and an end.

It is also in mid-life that men begin to see death as a kind of escape hatch, the ace up their sleeves. This is not to say that it does not occur at earlier times in man's life, but then it is very infrequent; however, when the pressures of life begin to mount and the theme of hopelessness finds its way into a person's mind, he may begin to try to toy with the ultimate cop-out. A leap off the bridge would silence all the mouths of the creditors, would put an end to the chronic pain, would erase the loneliness of a man's existence, would teach the husband who had left his wife for somebody else. In the interplay of these thoughts, it rarely occurs to the person to consider the meaning of this business in which he is about to engage. Perhaps in all of his days he has never considered the meaning of life. Does life have any meaning at all beyond the obscure fables that his mind may have only obliquely entertained? He asks these questions: If I am a creature, is it possible that there is a Creator? And if there is one, is it possible that He is accessible through some form of communication? If, then, there is a God, maybe he should step back from the edge of the bridge and give this whole subject further consideration. In the frenzy of what he is doing he hardly has time to waste on a subject he barely had time for when all systems were go.

I have never been convinced that the act of suicide is anything else but the final expression of a subtle psychotic process that began as an option and grew into a powerful force that seduced the person's mind. The most powerful instinct that man has is that of self-preservation. To destroy one's self goes against all of the forces of nature. To surmount the process of nature takes a force of such magnitude that it has to be either psychotic or demonic. A healthy human mind could not perpetuate such a perverse deed.

To those people who have suffered long and painful illnesses, death becomes a release from a torture chamber. To these people, the act of death is kind, but if, in those years of pain, all they could think about was their personal comfort, what a terrible waste of time. What sadness that, in all of those awful hours, their minds were not stimulated to consider the meaning of their existence. Were they ashamed of thoughts that would lead them to the possibility of life beyond this one? Did they feel that they would offend an intellect that scorned the mysticism of faith and found solace only in the chilly exactness of scientific thinking? I do not mean to demean scientific thinking. My mind was conditioned for many years by its tenets. The scientific method is the only way to understand the mechanics of physical phenomena. I do not, however, believe that it holds the answer to all of the problems of mankind. I consider man a tripartite being. To try to understand man's spiritual nature by employing scientific methods, which we use in the laboratories, would be as incongruous as trying to pick up an atom with ice tongs.

In a recent article concerning death, Sir MacFarlane Burnet, the 1960 co-winner of the Nobel Prize of medicine, makes this remarkable statement concerning the process of death. "In the end we die, and for us it is as if we had never been." This rather simplistic, but at the same time arrogant, statement from this learned man seems to epitomize the opinion of many men of science. The real tragedy of that statement is that a brilliant man, who spent half his life studying the wonders of nature from its microscopic depths to its macroscopic heights, could find no more meaning in the whole wonderful panorama of life than a process that began in birth and ended in an enigmatic experience called death. Some people might be piqued by the use of the word *arrogant* in reference to Sir MacFarlane's statement. I do not feel the word is in the least inappropriate. For in his statement, he categorically condemns all of the considerations of theologians and philosophers who have pondered these matters for centuries and insist that the process of life, which began here on earth, shall continue on into a more permanent form of life.

If life is what Sir MacFarlane Burnet suggests it is, then life is a

cosmic joke. Man's existence is the plaything of some eternal
spectator who allows man to participate in this meaningless
charade until the action becomes tedious, and then the spectator
pulls the curtain to pass on to a new act that may be more
stimulating.

Not everyone can be as cavalier about death as Doctor Burnet.
Most people fear its icy tentacles, its grim finality. To me the most
awful aspect of death is its silence. The lines of communication
have been severed. The memories live on, but the immediate
response of communication with the person is gone. You can ring
that telephone all day and night—but nobody's going to pick up
the receiver. Maybe that silence has a message and that message
is that this life is not the whole story. We are only going to be here
for a limited period of time. Perhaps we had better begin to think
about life and its significance, for, someday, somebody will ring
our phones night and day and there will not be an answer because
we will have taken up residence in another place. The message of
the finality of death is not the simple and arrogant conclusion that
says, "That's all there is so toss the body in the hole and shovel in
the dirt and let's get moving on to more important things." The
message that makes more sense to me is that the beautiful experience called life is a brief one, but it is not without meaning. All
around us we have evidence of the creative force that signifies
that life is certainly something more than a "tale told by an idiot
. . . signifying nothing."

Death then, is an important part of man's life. It is the mark of
his mortal finitude. A passage we must all make someday unless
Christ comes first. It delivers to us a message—one to which we
can apply our own interpretation—but it underscores the briefness of our stay. Even halfway up the mountain is not a long time.
As we get deeper into the middle years, we are amazed by the
fleetness of time and the tenuous quality of life itself.

When we were younger, as we previously discussed, death
usually seemed to be something that happened to other people,

people who were remote to us in age and acquaintance. As we begin to move up the mountain to middle life we hear of more and more people of our own age who have fallen beneath the scythe of the grim reaper. So the message gets louder and clearer. At the same time our defenses get stronger and stronger. The defense, again, most heavily relied upon, is denial. Death can happen to everybody else in the world, but it is not going to touch me. This message of invincibility is always appealing to the human ear, but as we move on into our sixties and seventies, the message sounds less viable. Even so, many people hang on to a thin thread of immortality until the very end.

People who do not know Christ can believe only the hard-boiled existential acceptance of death as something that happens to everybody. Unconsciously people bear a deep resentment to this cruel visitor who can come unasked at any time, but there is no way to express that resentment or to compensate for it unless it is in the act of ignoring it.

In mid-life, the Christian should begin to see death from a different perspective. He will always hold the instinctual fear that all human beings have for anything unknown, but he will not hide from it as do so many members of the human race. To most people death is the end of everything for the individual. Molecular particles will continue to exist in the genetic contribution that he has made to his children, but he or she, as an individual, will no longer exist.

To the Christian, however, death is, in some ways, the pinnacle of his earthly existence, for it is at the moment of death that the Christian will know whether all that he believes is true or false. At that time, faith will be nonexistent. All of the scales of ignorance will be removed from his eyes and the mysteries of man's life will be wiped away forever.

What a joyous moment that will be, when he will be reunited with all of his loved ones who have gone on before! When, once more, the lines of communication will be reestablished, the old voices heard again, and the deathly silence at last broken forever—no more goodbyes, no more quick slipping away of loved ones into the mysterious enigma of death.

The most glorious anticipation of the Christian is that, at the time of death, he will come face-to-face with his blessed Lord, his wonderful, patient Redeemer, who all of those years continued to love him in spite of the countless times the man ignored Him and went his willful way. At death, with its immediate launching into a new life, his relationship with Christ will be different. He will see Him with the same clarity that the disciple saw Him on the road to Damascus. He will not be meeting someone new, but rather Someone with whom he has been intimate, more intimate than with any other person. For only Christ can share all of the moments of our lives. It is good for us to remember that the Lord is with us, not only at those times when we feel close to Him, but also at those times when we ignore Him as though He did not exist. He is not only with us at the heights of our goodness, but at the very depths of our evilness. In the words of the Psalmist, "Whither shall I go from thy spirit? or whither shall I flee from thy presence? If I ascend up into heaven, thou art there: if I make my bed in hell, behold, thou art there." (Psalms 139:7, 8.) Once we accept Him as our redeemer, Christ is with us every step of the way. So we will not be encountering a stranger, but the best and the most intimate friend that we have ever had. When we think of death as a time of revelation and reunion, we immediately remove its venom. We can say with the Apostle Paul, "O death where is thy sting? O grave, where is thy victory?" (1 Corinthians 15:55.) That does not mean that Christians should giggle at funerals or feel a kind of superiority over the rest of mankind because Christians have an answer that overcomes the supposedly inevitable victory of death. There is a very human part of every Christian that can identify with the loss of a bereaved one. Did not the Lord Himself weep at the funeral of Lazarus even though He knew through His eternal omniscience that Lazarus was to rise again very soon in a miraculous way? It is a sad fact that many Christians, who know of the superiority they have over death through Christ, feel a kind of aloofness and distance from those who do not have the same kind of assurance. This is a sign of the most flagrant form of immaturity. The Lord never flaunted His superiority in any relationship that He had with other human beings. The young woman caught in the act of adultery found no pity in her ring of accusers, young or old, but the Lord, able to see that her depravity was no worse than that of her stiff-necked, self-righteous accusers, was able, through His wisdom, to free her from her accusers and to make her feel within her heart the intense warmth of His love. Christians should never feel superior to any human frailty. What must characterize our lives is the same sympathy that Christ could feel for any kind of human weakness. This kind of maturity can only come in a person who allows the Holy Spirit to work freely and unhindered in his life. This requires a communion that is steady, a moment-by-moment sharing of life and death with the Lord. Paul says that we should pray without ceasing. Paul knew that that goal was not really totally possible in a human being, but if total communion is our goal, then we are assured of a significant partial communion. The more we open our lives in all of its dimensions to Christ, the more our lives begin to reflect His Person.

Death has another significance in the Christian life. Paul says, "I die daily." (*See* 1 Corinthians 15:31.) The apostle is not referring to a physical death, but rather to a psychological and spiritual death of the old self. The old man was formed in a mind devoid of the knowledge of Christ's love for him personally. His basic attitudes and opinions were colored by all of the prejudices of the society in which he was raised. His motivations were tainted with fear and greed. Even his righteousnesses were as Isaiah proclaimed, "as filthy rags." (*See* Isaiah 64:6.) This is the part of the reborn person that must die as the Christian moves into the middle years. He should feel the effect of that death. With each new day, and therefore with each new death, the Christian, who is maturing, should actually feel the dimming of the old man with all of his destructive impulses. His mind should become more and more in tune with the Holy Spirit. Physical death is a one-time occurrence, but the spiritual and emotional death of the old self is something that continues daily until the person leaves this scene through physical death. Daily death to the old life is something that is absolutely necessary for the growth of the Christian.

Freud referred to another death form that is more akin to the multiple deaths of which we have just been speaking. He referred to the death instinct. This is the unconscious psychological force that is in direct opposition to the positive life forces within the person's mind. Many of Freud's postulates were based upon physical models. The forces that operate in the human body are either designed for anabolism—the building up of the person's body—or catabolism—the breaking down of the body parts. The forces of anabolism and catabolism are in dynamic balance and, as long as a person lives, the life forces dominate the flow of the equation. As we increase with age, the balance of the vital equation shifts so that the energy flow becomes more negative. This is understandable in a finite body where the ultimate condition is physical dissolution.

Freud believed that this same kind of polarity existed within the mind. The forces that operate within our minds are constructive or destructive like the forces of anabolism and catabolism. They are positive or negative. The forces are unconscious and, therefore, are not directly accessible to our wills, but the manifestation of these forces is clearly discernible in our conscious awareness. For example, I may intend to cut the front lawn because it is beginning to look more like a pasture than the neatly manicured lawns of the other people in the neighborhood; however, I may never get around to the job until the snow falls in November. The death force—counterproductive—manifested itself in the endless rationalizations that formed the substance of my procrastination.

Our minds are riddled with negative forces that Freud described as the monolithic death force. They impede our growth as positive, productive human beings. They are indeed the very substance of that old self that should die in the life of the maturing Christian.

Perhaps one more thought on death would be worth our consideration. It was through the death of one Man that the availability of eternal life came to mankind. We have talked of millions of deaths of single individuals and the billions of multiple deaths within the mind of the maturing Christian, but the one single death of Christ gave death a new meaning to mankind. For to the believer, as we indicated above, it meant a new life—a life of certainty, joy, and peace, free of the loneliness that plagues all of mankind.

The Lord asked us not to remember His life, but rather His death. From the human perspective that request may seem morbid and unproductive, but the Lord left us with this request that we might be strengthened spiritually.

It is only in the contemplation of His death that we can begin to appreciate the enormity of His love for us. Christ, "Who is the image of the invisible God, the firstborn of every creature," (Colossians 1:15) the Creator of all living things, was willing to go through death—a condition that was diametrically opposite to all that for which He stood—to reconcile sinners to God.

It is impossible for man to appreciate the depths of Christ's love for us by a single contemplation of His death. It is only through multiple recollections and, therefore, identifications with His death through the Holy Spirit, that we can begin to appreciate, in even the smallest way, all that Christ did for us. We contemplate His death, but not with the sadness and confusion of that group of disciples who refused to believe that Christ would die in the manner that He tried to prepare them for many times. We can look back at that death with a clarity that was not available to them. We see it not as the cruel end of a good man, a shameful example of the most extreme form of injustice, but rather the majestic portal that leads to glory for all of those who believe in its power of reconciliation. There is a beauty in that death that was concealed from His disciples. There is no special talent of intellect that would cause one person to see the significance of that death more clearly than anyone else. Its beauty comes to us only through repeated exposure. That is why in mid-life the person, who may have known Christ since his younger years, begins to feel within himself a growing sense of intimacy with his Lord because of the repeated exposure to His death.

How strange these words must seem to the person who does not acknowledge Christ as his Redeemer, one who can only see Him as a good man who was the victim of the cruelest form of injustice. How sad that they will never know a form of love that is completely unilateral and does not depend for its integrity on a reciprocal love with the other person.

Death then is something that comes to every man unless he is redeemed, and Christ returns first. It is a lonely experience, the contemplation of which brings fear to the heart of every man. It is a remote phenomenon in the early years of a man's existence, happening to people much older or distant in some other way. The theme comes in stronger in young adult life. Sometimes friends are quickly terminated in ghastly accidents, comrades are blown away by the ravages of war. It is in mid-life that the sombre strain can no longer be denied. The middle-aged person no longer sees death as something that can happen to other people, but as something that can happen to him. To man in his finite condition this is a very frightening realization, for life is all he has and when he is gone, as Sir MacFarlane Burnet declares with all his scientific honesty, "It is as though he had never been." What a contrast to the Christian's view of death as both the entrance into a new life of eternal dimension and the climax of his life of faith, when he finally meets his Lord face-to-face!

We discussed Paul's concept of perpetual death in First Corinthians in his statement, "I die daily." Here we see death as a growth factor. Death to the old self is like pulling the weeds in the garden so the flowers can grow to their fullest potential.

We also touched on Freud's idea of death instinct—the negative force in man's mind, the instinct directly related to the advent of sin in man's life as the result of his rebellion in the Garden of Eden. And then finally, the significance of that one death of Christ's that offered eternal life to all men who accepted Christ as their Saviour.

It is in middle life that man is first able to see the varied aspects of death. It is through the understanding and accepting of death in all of its meanings that man can go on to full maturity in his human and Christian life, redeeming each moment as a very precious gift from God.

6
Marriage

Most marriages begin in the most ideal circumstances. Two beautiful, healthy, young people, drawn together by all of the forces that make them human, vow a life together that will last through thick and thin, until death do them part. They do not speak these words idly—from the time that they both speak them, they mean every word. They see their future together only in terms of continuing enrichment. This is only the beginning. It is obvious to them that, in the embrace of their mutual commitment, their love for one another will grow deeper and deeper. The negative side of the human relationship never enters their minds, or, if it does, it doesn't last long, for the intensity of the positive forces of their love quickly rolls over it as a billow of the sea submerges an obtrusive rock. Not long after their explosive love settles, their mutual enchantment retreats before the forces of reality. Before the marriage they saw each other only in the pure, if not unreal, light of idealism. Their relationship was characterized by a mutual obsession with one another that intruded itself into every moment of their lives. It was necessary to be with each other as much as possible; to touch and to look at one another; to spend long hours together often saying nothing, but locked in a physical, emotional vise that molded them together in a relationship transcending time and often propriety.

The intensity of that first phase of the marriage relationship was so strong for most people that all of the things that followed in their lives were anticlimactic. When one starts a journey from the ultimate peak, there is only one way to go and that is down. The decrescendo begins for a couple as they gradually see sides of one another's personalities that were obscured in the brilliant glow of premarital expectations. Dispositions that may have been highly inflammatory in other personal relationships were subdued by the need to maintain the positive flow of love. Camelot had to be maintained at all costs.

Soon after the honeymoon is over, when the meals are served, not in the glamorous setting of the bridal suite of a Bermuda hotel but in the drab uncurtained kitchen of a sparsely furnished apartment that needs painting in the worst way, the dispositions begin to gravitate to the more natural level of lability. The soft, often purring answers, in conversations so characteristic of premarital communication, give way to short monosyllabic bursts of petulance. Long gaps of silence often punctuate these fiery dialogues. Fights are frequent, often involving the efficiency of the wife's cooking and other household duties or with the husband's general sloppiness around the home and his tendency to want to be out with the boys more than his wife wants him to be. Not infrequently, the wife will go to visit Mother for a few days for some moral support. And husband, left alone in the dreary apartment, spends more time out with the boys and eats his meals at the corner restaurant.

Most people work their way through those traumatic early years. Their marriages fall into some kind of stable order—the result of silent compromises producing a situation that is compatible to both people in most of their relationships with one another.

There are, of course, people who never recover from the first posthoneymoon shock. The intense feeling of love they felt before the marriage is replaced by an equally intense hatred. These marriages rarely survive for people in their twenties. Such marriages, in midlife, would produce unions of psychotic proportions, held together by the grim forces of insanity, which the French refer to as *folie á deux*—the madness of two.

After the first four or five years of marriage, the children come along. These tiny creatures on the planet Earth do profound things to the people who created them. How mystified the parents are as they look down upon those tiny replicas of themselves. How strange they appear in one respect and yet how familiar in another.

The infant will become a subtle tyrant in the mother's life. The needs of the child will determine the mother's behavior. All of her activities will be affected by this tiny despot, who for a few years will demand almost all of her attention. The child becomes the central theme of her life. The previous altercations between the husband and the wife lose their intensity as the priority system changes. It is always easier to deal with problems of lesser priority. Unfortunately, the shift in her priority system will come back to haunt her at a later date when the children are gone and she is left living with a comparative stranger.

The husband, too, gains, but also loses, because of the children. He is thankful for their appearance in the home because they will serve as something to occupy his wife's mind and at the same time get her off his back, but his financial responsibility to the family increases.

So we see developing in the home a curious dichotomy. On the one hand, the forces of responsibility deepen the legal commitment these people have made to one another. Each of them, in his own way, is made more and more aware of that responsibility. Because of the increasing material needs of the family, it becomes increasingly important for the husband to be successful at his work, so he spends more time at work. He brings home material that he could not deal with at the office because he spent too much time on the phone. While the family, including his wife, is in the family room watching television, he is closeted in the library doing some homework so he can get the jump on Joe Blow, who is breathing down his neck at the office. The kids and Mom get used to Dad's going into solitary confinement. Mother has times of resentment, when she misses the lack of adult companionship, but she sees it most of the time as a necessary evil. After all, you cannot run a station wagon on tap water or feed hungry mouths with good intentions.

The other half of the dichotomy is that this fouled-up value system drives these people further and further away from each other emotionally. They are both increasingly aware of the children's problems, but less and less aware of the problem that exists between them as people, who on one fatal day of their lives before a crowd of witnesses made some rather serious vows to one another. What occurs is that each digs his own hole deeper and deeper so, when the time comes for the reunion that occurs in middle life, they are so deeply involved in their respective holes that they cannot even see the other person's head. A solid block of emotional earth exists between them. Their only hope of reconciliation is for them to climb out of their respective holes and try, after all those years of silence, to communicate with one another. It is not easy, for human beings are creatures of habit. All of our metabolic and mental systems operate on the basis of homeostasis. That is, once they reach an equilibrium, they resist any change to that state even though the existing state may be counterproductive.

One of the things that they may not have been aware of through the years is the way that they began to use the children as instruments of manipulation. The mother, of course, is in a position of advantage as far as using the children as ploys. It is quite clear to see that the raising of the children is her prime responsibility. In terms of actual exposure, she is far ahead of her spouse. Whereas he may see the children in those early years for two or three hours a day, Mother is in touch with them during all of their waking hours. The husband's time with the children is brief. Many men leave the house before the children begin to stir and return after the children have gone to bed. Dad is really only an effectual member of the family, as far as the children are concerned, on the weekend. Even then he is often an elusive figure—compulsively engaged with chores around the house or involved with golf or tennis as he satisfies his needs for healthy, competitive relationships with his contemporaries but ignores the responsibility of sharing time with his own family. When his wife reminds him of irresponsible behavior with a voice that trembles and a face that hardly disguises her anger and resentment, he recoils with an anger of his own. He sees her behavior as clear evidence of her attempts to emasculate him and convert him into a Mr. Milquetoast. So the emotional gap widens. She sees him as someone who does not want to grow up, a boy who wants to go on being a high-school sophomore forever.

The children cannot help noticing this poorly disguised dissention. This highly charged situation is a real threat to their emotional security. They are bothered by the unexplainable contention between the two authoritative figures in their lives. Their loyalties are divided. They may see Father in a very positive light—the nice guy who works so hard all week and plays on the weekend. They do not mind his tennis or golf because they play games too. In their secret hearts, they would much rather play games with their friends than with Dad, who only has half his heart in it anyway. They really cannot understand why Mom complains so much. He does not seem all that bad and, too, he never reacts to their infractions in the same way that she does. He tends to be easy on them. It may never occur to them that this equanimity may be based upon the fact that he may be many miles away at the time of the trouble. When he hears about it, a large amount of time has ticked away. He cannot get as excited about it as Mother did at the time of the crisis. And so, halfway through her discourse about Johnny's infraction, Dad's eyes begin to wander and his hand goes to his mouth to stifle a yawn. He is tired, so understandably his guard is down. Mother, meanwhile, who is beginning to lose confidence in her ability to present this incident in its full emotional impact, feels as if she has been dealt a mortal blow. It is quite clear to her that this deceitful playboy, who is sitting across from her, is completely bored with what she is saying. He is like an extra child in the family, only he is the most incorrigible of all because he should know better. She rises from the chair and leaves the room in disgust. To the guilty party, who just happened to be walking by the door at that time, she makes a sarcastic remark about his father, who from now on is going to take care of all the discipline in the house because she has abdicated.

So Father takes the boy into the library and spanks him with a gusto that goes far beyond his intention. The child senses the inappropriateness. For indeed 70 percent of the intensity of Daddy's blows had nothing to do with Junior's crime at all, but was an act of anger against his emasculating wife, who has no understanding at all. Father hopes that a good night's sleep will get things back into perspective. As soon as the alarm clock rings in the morning, he is up from his bed like a man shot from a cannon. He heads for the bathroom where he shaves and showers—Phase I of the launching procedure that will get him on the 7:37 train for New York. Mother, too, under the influence of Pavlovian instincts that have bypassed her conscious mind, hurries to wash and get down to the kitchen to prepare for the hungry children who will descend upon her in no time. About halfway through soft-boiling the eggs, her mind begins to clear. She remembers with increasing clarity the awful incident in the library the previous night. Bitterness begins to seep into her mind, contaminating all of her thoughts and actions. Too late, she realizes the eggs have boiled over and will be as hard as rubber balls. The plates and silverware are banged on the table with aggressive abandon. By the time the children swarm into the room, her temper is at the breaking point. The husband, with primitive hope in his heart that all will be well, looks over the kitchen scene, and immediately all of the red lights go on inside of his head. This is no place for man or beast. He grabs a quick cup of coffee, tries to kiss his wife good-bye but only succeeds in kissing the air behind her fast-turning head. That is enough for him. So, with his morning paper tucked under his arm, he yells good-bye to the kids and bolts out the front door toward his place of refuge on the commuter train that will take him into the big city, far removed from the goblins and witches that inhabit the suburbs.

It is under the influence of this kind of crisis that strange things begin to happen in the minds of many people in the early stages of middle age. We see them veering off in divergent directions. The man sees the home as a place he is obliged to go to because of financial responsibilities and perhaps, to a lesser degree, a moral obligation to his children and wife. He does not look upon his home as a place of comfort and solace where he can bring his troubles and get a sympathetic ear. The only troubles allowed to be discussed at home are those of his wife's. So he learns to listen, but not always successfully, because thoughts of more pleasant things and people crowd his mind.

The office, as we have suggested before, has become a refuge to him. There he is respected for the increasing efficiency of his work. His secretary treats him as the most important person in the world. She brings him a cup of coffee at the exact moment he needs it. She hangs on his every word as though he were a prophet. His word commands her immediate and willing action. He begins to share personal things with her, which she guards with her life. He begins to look forward to coming to the office. He wonders what new ensemble she will have on today. He wonders how such a young girl can have enough money to buy outfits from Saks Fifth Avenue and Lord and Taylor's. He begins to dread the weekends. They seem so pointless, so barren. It is as though he has to take part in some tedious drama he does not have the heart for. He thinks, with dread, about the hundred and one things he needs to do around the home. The lawn is beginning to look like a wheat field because the mower is broken down. He wonders why his wife does not call the repair man and get it fixed. She is around the house all week. What else has she got to do? He looks out the window at the wheat field and shrugs his shoulder. Maybe there will be an early fall this year and the grass will not grow anymore. So he turns away from the window and heads for the television set. There he sits all afternoon telling the greatest quarterbacks in the business how they should run their football teams. Or maybe he is one of the braver ones who, with set face, heads out the front door with his golf clubs in tow. He waves to his wife who is outside raking leaves. Salutations are stiff and formal. You would think they were perfect strangers. He drives out of the driveway just a little too fast, spreading gravel all over the freshly raked lawn. She stares at him with something that approaches cold hatred. She throws the rake down on the pile of leaves and retreats to the bedroom where she quietly cries herself to sleep.

That night at the country club, he notices that she is drinking a little too much. Her conversation does not make any sense. She begins to put her arm around men in an indiscriminate way. He senses their embarrassment as they look at other members of the group with raised eyebrows and very soon manage stiff retreat to the safe environments of their wives. She becomes inappropriately loud. She demands attention as she thrusts her maudlin ideas on a group of people who wish that her husband would take her home. It becomes quite obvious that this is the only option left to him. With some help from his best friend's wife, he gets her coat on and escorts her out the door. The drive home is quiet except for her off-key humming of some indistinguishable tune. The husband is locked in silence. This evening is yet another incident in a series of happenings that are beginning to take a definite pattern in their lives. He longs for the 7:37 train that will carry him away from the horror of this charade and to the enchanted island of Manhattan. There, amongst its golden spires, he will be met in the "throne room" of his office by a beautiful young princess who will stand before him dressed in her Bergdorf Goodman creation and hand him a cup of steaming hot coffee. Suddenly his revery is broken by the loud, garrulous voice of the person riding beside him. "Where are you going, stupid? You've missed the turnoff to our road!"

The things that are going on in the mind of the woman during this stage of her life are quite different from those of the man. She may have been a college woman, a person whose mind was trained to be sensitive to social and political issues, or her interests may have been in literature, art, or music. In the early days of marriage, she may have been able to get to the museum on Friday and have lunch with her husband at one of the better cafes. She may have managed her budget so that they could see a play every once in a while. Those were romantic days when they could do things like going to the mountain for the weekend. But, again, even in those days, she had to deal with large chunks of boredom.

Or maybe in those early years, she had to work to support him in graduate school. Secretly she enjoyed being able to continue to work. She knew that she absolutely had to do this or her husband's tuition would not be paid. There were, however, times when she resented it, especially when the boss dropped a huge pile of work on her desk at three o'clock in the afternoon and told her that he wanted it done that day. It may, too, have rankled her a bit when she saw her friends buying new cars and refrigerators and even buying houses, when she had to ride the bus, live in rented rooms, and pinch every penny she could get. She knew that some day, when her husband was a lawyer, she would live in a colonial home in some fashionable neighborhood, drive a Mercedes, and belong to the country club. The most important factor in her life, at that time, was that she had a raison d'être. Her husband needed her in a very practical way. She knew he could not make it without her.

In the process of time, things change. When children come into the scene, as we have previously indicated, they put financial pressures on the husband that make him grind even harder at his work. In many ways this little extra pressure for him is a bonus. It simply strengthens his inherent ambitions. It gives him a justifiable reason for spending more time at the office, but for her, it provides a greater necessity to be at home. All of her social engagements must be secondary to the needs of the children. They become her sole criterion in making any social decision. As the result of that, her social engagements are modified to near extinction. She may, in a moment of repose, long for a lunch at the Plaza, a ballet at Lincoln Center, or just some time to stroll through the stores along Fifth Avenue. She must quickly dispel these fantasies. They may be reconstructed in the future, but now she must tend to the business at hand. The suppression of these desires is always associated with an increment of resentment which will erupt at some time in the future.

In the early years, the children are completely dependent upon her. They actually need her to survive. As they grow older, they need her in a less elemental way. At some time, they learn to dress themselves. They no longer have to be led to school by the guiding hand of Mother, who can negotiate crossing streets better than they can. Now they can look both ways just as carefully as Mother does. They begin to enjoy their growing sense of responsibility, but the independence of the children is very often a real threat to the mother. The less the children need her, the more time she has to reflect upon other aspects of her life. The growing schism between her and her husband can no longer be avoided. She has more time to think about it. Many mothers deal with the element of the children's independence by sabotaging it. They attempt to stretch that time of dependency just as far as they can. Some succeed in stretching certain aspects of it for a lifetime.

In those early years of raising the children, the husband has become less significant in her life. He has gone his way, she has gone hers. The time of their exposure to one another becomes increasingly brief—more a matter of duty than pleasure. Their real worlds seldom touch. She has no idea of the problems that he has at the office. She sees them as much less complicated than hers. She knows he has no idea of the amount of frustration associated with her work. She thinks being a stockbroker would be fun—lunch out every noon at the fanciest restaurants, getting involved with deals that concern millions of dollars, associating with glamorous clientele. She has nowhere near the freedom he does. He gets on the train and rides away from the real problems of life. She has noticed his increasing aloofness, as though by some curious metamorphosis he was becoming more superior. Part of her resentment is in the realization that, as the years go by, her job seems to lose its importance, whereas his seems to become more important. She does not get a dime for her work, but each year, he seems to be paid more and more. It does not seem fair. So the theme of injustice enters her thinking. She, indeed, may become an injustice collector.

She ultimately sees herself as a victim of inexorable forces over which she has no control. Her whole life becomes an excuse for not living. Depressive forces that could possibly go on to pathological dimensions enter her mind. The villain, of course, is that stranger who darts out of the house quickly in the morning and who comes home later and later at night. As long as the children are in the house, she can contend with the situation. It is when the kids move out that an entirely new ball game begins for both parties. What has happened through the years is that two Dr. Frankensteins have created two different monsters. The monster the wife builds is the colossal egocentric husband—totally absorbed in his own activities, immature, self-centered, interested only in his own pursuits, completely unfeeling and unknowledgeable about his wife and her needs. He sees her only as a person who has, in the past few years, become increasingly inaccessible, shallow, and out of touch with the real issues of life. He becomes increasingly sensitive to her growing feeling of bitterness that he reads in the increasing lines of her face, her constant put-down of everything of importance to him. She has become an obstacle in his life—an albatross around his neck.

As time goes on, bitterness is returned with bitterness. Their relationship becomes exsanguinated, for all the spontaneity in life has left it. It is easy to nurse the resentments of other people when you are preoccupied with other things. The deadliness of this indifference seems less lethal when you are involved with the problems of teenage children. The shrewishness of your wife seems less threatening when you come home to a house full of rambunctious kids. When the buffers are gone and you have to deal with the other person in the starkness of direct confrontation, there is no place to hide. The issues have to be dealt with in the open. Like two strangers who meet in the darkness of a lonely street—each afraid of the other—they see the other person only in terms of being the obstacle to their happiness, the cause of all of the things that went wrong in their lives. At a time in their lives when their love should be most mellow, they feel only a coldness, a lack of respect, in many instances a hatred. Their love, which began with such burning intensity, has turned to ashes. There is nothing left but memories—even these are vague and pointless. Their relationship has been a double-barreled failure. Their only meaningful relation is their children. Their only way out seems to be a parting of the ways, but even this is impossible for they see the other person as someone whose only purpose in life is to cheat and humiliate them.

Yes, marriage in middle life can be very bleak—the tragic end of a misbegotten dream. In all too many instances, this is the case. The pressures of an increasingly complex world make it very difficult to maintain any kind of stability in a relationship as demanding as that of marriage. Yet we know that marriage is the most stable relationship that can be achieved between a man and a woman.

As we previously indicated, one of the real problems of the process of marriage is that it begins at too lofty a plane. It begins at what, in too many instances, is the zenith of the relationship. All movements from then on are down. Too many people think that there is something magical in the marriage yoke. All of us were raised on stories about the beautiful princess and the handsome prince who, after many fiery trials, were finally married and lived happily ever after. What the expression "and lived happily ever after" seems to signify is that once you are married, all that lies before you is eternal bliss. How greatly the myth fades in the light of reality. That is not to suggest that marriages all wind down and are doomed to miserable failure as we so often see. The marriage relationship offers more opportunity for real joy than any other human relationship, but that joy does not materialize like a rabbit out of a hat. The two beautiful people, who began at a delicate peak, must realize that the enormous attraction they felt at the beginning of their relationship is the momentum they need to carry them through some of the rocky shoals that lie ahead. At the beginning of their relationship, each one was overwhelmed by the positive factors in the other person. This does not mean that he or she completely overlooked the negative dimensions in the other person. It was simply a case of being so totally focused on the things each one wanted to see about the other person that the things he did not want to see were formless objects in the periphery of his vision—things that would be washed away when the floodgates of their love were finally open.

When that other side of marriage begins to rear its ugly head, couples at first are shocked. It is like the child finding the toys in Mommy's closet before Christmas. We all love that jolly fat man with snow-white whiskers and round tummy that used to wiggle down our chimneys even though we did not have any. We hated to give up believing in him. He was always so good to us. The generosity of Mother and Father paled in comparison with that of the jolly fat man. We learned to accept the truth even though the truth has less luster than the myth. In fact, as life went on we may have come to the point of understanding that the giving of the gift involved more than a little sacrifice on the part of the giver. We never considered that aspect of Santa's giving. We were introduced to a new dimension of giving that made the whole process so much richer.

In like manner, at the beginning of the marriage, the relationship may be very lofty but not very deep. Depth is achieved by digging, not a very dignified form of occupation but one that gives stability to a relationship that might otherwise be too top-heavy.

The mutual possessiveness, so characteristic of the honeymoon, produces an emotional high that may never again be realized. Many people associate the emotional factor with love. To them love is a feeling—the more the feeling, the greater the love, but, as we shall see in another part of the book, love involves many more facets than emotion. The intensity of that possessiveness not only produces an emotional high, it, at the same time, produces a low in terms of personal relationships with other people. In the premarital and honeymoon period, couples are only happy when they are together. The desire to be with other people is at a minimal level. As the relationship matures, the intensity of that mutual possessiveness diminishes. The desire to be with other people increases. The movement away from that point of intensity is interpreted, by many people, as a form of rejection. There is an infantile factor in that initial relationship that demands that this uterine-like possessiveness be extended to all phases of their lives. They cannot see that these infantile attitudes sabotage the development of mature love—one that respects the individuality of the other person. This respect is reinforced by a trust that allows that love to grow even though the loved one may be involved in activities that separate him from the other person.

Statistics bear out the fact that, in our society, the complexities which grow each year and the moral substance which is continually being eroded by a perverted sense of freedom, cause many marriages to seldom last to middle age. If they do, they resemble anything but a love relationship. Some are cold-blooded business transactions—two people locked together because it would be financially unfeasible for them to be otherwise. Others are total strangers, who hardly speak to one another. In each case, they are held together by force of habit and the fear of change, at an age when any kind of change is threatening. Some braver souls hold together until the children are fully grown, and then each goes his separate way like ships that pass in the night. Some stay together because of the religious tradition that was planted in their minds in early childhood and which remains through all the days of their lives, anchored down by the powerful sinews of guilt and fear.

What a far cry these pathetic relationships are compared to the rich ones that God had in mind when He instituted the act of marriage in the Garden of Eden. Two souls become one. That oneness seems to imply a growing sense of understanding of the other person. The more one understands the other person, the less threatened one is by the individuality of the other. One partner supports the developing of the other's talents to the fullest degree even if the development means periods of separation. This is such a difficult concept for human beings to accept. They may agree to it intellectually, but, on those lonely nights, after the wife has been left with the children three days in a row, her trust wears thin. Thoughts of injustice creep into her mind. She tries to fight it off, but the sore lump grows in her throat. At some point, she cannot hold back any longer and bursts into tears. She hates herself for it. She knows her action is weak and saturated with self-pity. The concept begins to lose its validity. The whole thing seems awfully unfair. It does not take much effort to develop that theme. Before very long, the marriage seems in great jeopardy. How fragile then are marriages even between two intelligent, emotionally mature people, who are willing to work on their marriage and yet find the forces of doubt and fear too much to contend with!

It is only the Christian who has the opportunity to experience the joy of a fully mature marriage. As we have seen above, human nature allows the marriage to grow only to limited specifications. The uncertainties of finite experience are too great for human love to ignore the menacing shadows of doubt and uncertainty. Human relationships are based upon reciprocal principles. If I love you, I expect you to love me. If that reciprocal relationship does not exist, then the relationship is doomed to failure.

Christian marriages are consolidated not only on the basis of reciprocal love, but to a greater extent by the common unilateral relationship each participant has with the Lord Jesus Christ. It is the unilateral spiritual love that is the greatest adhesive force in their relationship. Christ loved each of us long before we were even aware of Him. His love for us does not depend to the slightest degree upon our love for Him. It is only a love of this kind that can transcend the pressures of finite existence. It must seem strange to the world that our love for His Person should increase and enrich our love for others.

This is not to suggest that, because Christian marriages have within them the potential for a mature love relationship, such a relationship automatically materializes. Christians have to work hard on their marriages like other human beings. The most important principle in the Christian's marriage, as in all Christian relationships, is that Christ should always have the supreme priority. Anything that comes between the Lord and the individual will be destroyed. How many times, for example, have I seen a Christian marriage ruined because the wife put the wayward husband (or vice versa) between herself and the Lord. In a perfectly human way, she allowed the growing bitterness that she felt toward her husband to crowd out any joy and peace that she might have had in her quiet time with the Lord. All the forces of negative thinking were allowed to move into her mind and strangle the positive forces of the Spirit. The more bitter she became, the greater were the forces of rationalization that nourished that bitterness. The process of rationalization led her inevitably to the conclusion that the only way their marriage could be salvaged was for her husband to change his attitudes. What she is really saying is that her relationship with Christ, in this particular matter, is essentially irrelevant. The only thing that is important is that her husband change. Any other suggestion is inadmissible.

It is in just this kind of circumstance that Christians can prove that they have a power that towers far above the powers of the world. In a situation, for example, where in mid-life the husband becomes increasingly remote, seems to care for nothing but himself, and treats his wife as if she were a piece of furniture, we can see that the husband is really the one who is at fault. His involvement with himself makes him less accessible to his family and especially to his wife. The wife is overwhelmed by the obvious unfairness of the situation. She does a quick personal inventory and comes to the understandable conclusion that, although she might not be perfect, nothing she has done deserves this kind of treatment. His nature, therefore, is totally unjustified. She, therefore, is justified in being angry and in accumulating as many accusations as she can against this heartless brute. The elaborations of his shortcomings become the driving compulsion of her life. His brutish effigy is at the apex of her existence. It is the consuming fire that tyrannizes her every movement. What she cannot see is that her pilgrimage of justice is taking her farther and farther away from the only One who could provide an answer to her problem. Her situation is impossible from a human point of view. She has every reason in the world to vent her anger against this outrage, but the more justifiable her case, the less accessible becomes her husband.

As the case against him grows greater and greater, he retreats more and more from the situation. The more defensive he becomes, the greater the need he has to see her only in the role of the dragon. From the human point of view, we are looking at a stalemate—the immovable object versus the irresistible force. What happens is that each person, convinced of the justice of his position, becomes entangled in his own righteousness. Seeing solutions in terms of what the other person has to do, he may try to persuade the person to be more objective, to see that, in every human relationship that fails, mistakes exist on both sides of the ledger. He may be rash enough to advise the person that he or she cannot do anything about the other person's contribution to the marriage, but only his own. It is a form of logic that is short-lived. It is quickly smothered by the hungry weeds of self-pity.

It is only the Christian, then, who has access to another way. If my relationship with Christ is the most important one in my life, then my relationship with any other person is subordinate. I can then begin to live with the imperfections in his life in the same way that Jesus did. He was not intimidated by the flaws in the character of the woman at the well, not because He was unaware of them, for he pointed some of them out to her. (*See* John 4:6–29.) His attitude to her weaknesses did not lead to condemnation. The woman had tried the love route. She had committed herself four times legally to different men. All had ended in failure. Maybe love without commitment would work or maybe she just settled on that one because all of the other relationships had failed. The woman obviously had the capacity to love, but there was something in the marriage relationship that she could not handle. Perhaps her demands for reciprocal love were too great. Maybe she overreacted to the sporadic rejections of her husbands. One thing is sure, she could not find in the marriage the security that she was looking for. I think it is very interesting that the Lord did not map out a ten-point psychological plan for her to use in stabilizing her relationship with her male companion. His conversation with her was primarily spiritual. The woman had some theological sensitivity: she knew that the Jews had no dealings with the Samaritans; furthermore, she had some familiarity with the patriarch Jacob at whose well they were drinking. She also knew that the fathers worshipped in that mountain, whereas, the Jews said that "in Jersulem is the place where men ought to worship." She was also aware that "Messiah cometh, which is called the Christ" and what the Lord was pointing out to the woman was that her life lacked an authentic spiritual dimension. She needed the living water that springs up into everlasting life. With that eternal dimension comes a new perspective, a new power and the things of this life become less binding. There is a freedom to deal with real problems that is just not possible from a finite point of view. What the Lord was telling this woman was that, if she drank the water *He* would give her, she would have something that would transcend any human circumstance— something as elemental as thirst or as complicated as marriage. In a very real sense the woman of Samaria was in the middle-life crisis. She had run out of husbands and was now involved with the most basic of all things, namely survival. What the Lord was saying to her was that, no matter what kind of problems she had, the first step in their resolution was to get herself into an authentic spiritual relationship with the One who could give her answers of eternal substance.

The world may have developed clever methods of dealing with marriages that have gone sour, but, in so many instances, they are like the armed truces worked out between warring nations. Neither wants to lay down the arms entirely because each would be too vulnerable. People can work out treaties where the terms permit that each do his own thing under certain limits. Such marriages are a travesty compared to the concept of marriage God had in mind for human beings. In a Christian marriage relationship, two people become one. This is a great mystery. Indeed, it is more than a mystery—to the world it is incomprehensible. How can two people become one without destroying their own personalities? Are people involved in an ideal marriage mutual yes-

men? agreeing on everything? never showing any individuality?
No! God made us all different for a reason. He never meant us to
surrender our unique qualities. Part of the incredible mystery of
marriage is that, even though the two people become one, they
hang on to their own individualities. That can only be achieved if
each person makes the primary relationship in life the one between himself and the Lord Jesus Christ. It is only when they put
the other person between themselves and Christ that they get into
trouble. It is inconceivable to me how two people, whose marriage relationship has been mutually destructive for twenty-five or
thirty years can ever change into one that is mutually constructive. The negative forces are too deeply etched in their minds.
The intellectual appeal of a positive relationship is swamped with
a flood of negative forces that have prevailed for such a long
period of time. It is only the living water, that is available at the
well that never runs dry, that overrides deficiencies of our finite
nature. It is only when a man can see himself the way the Lord
sees him that he is in a power position. God sees man in the
totality of his weakness. God can see beyond one's intellectual
defenses. God looks upon the heart, not on the outward man. In
those people who trust in Christ, God sees another dimension of
man. To God the man who has trusted Christ as Saviour is someone He loves so much that He was willing to give His only Son to
die for him. That is quite a price to pay for someone you love. The
Christian must be aware of his own weakness, but at the same
time the strength that he has through the fact that God loves him
so very much. The juxtaposition of these two ideas gives the
person that special attitude, only available to the Christian, that is
real humility linked with the awesome power of the Holy Spirit. It
is when the Christian is in that power position that the process of
regeneration can occur in any area of his life.

The saddest spectacle of all is to see Christians, who have this
power, ignore it as though it did not even exist. Some people have
faith enough to believe that Christ is their Redeemer, but cannot

fit Him into the nitty-gritty of daily life. We will talk in more detail about that elsewhere in this book, but it is a concept that bears repeating several times. How easy it is to turn off the spiritual component of our beings! But that is understandable because our first level of awareness is linked with our humanness. Our sensory mechanisms make us very much aware of this world. Our perceptual mechanisms tell us very little of the spiritual world. That world operates, as we have mentioned elsewhere, on the basis of faith. That is why people of the world have so much difficulty with spiritual matters. They cannot be captured by mathematical formulas. Spiritual forces go beyond the comfortable precision of scientific synthesis, but that is where the real power is—the deeper becomes our faith, the richer becomes our life. It is then that we have the power to deal with the deficiencies of our finite existence.

The Christian, whose marriage in mid-life has become a shambles through neglect, ambition, narcissism, or any of the other destructive forces man is vulnerable to, can see within his own life the wonderful transforming power of the Holy Spirit, for the power behind that Spirit is God's unilateral love. When that love works in the human heart, all of the monsters created by Frankenstein-like characters melt away as wax effigies before the sun. All those injustices, so close to the surface of the mind, fade away like the dreams of childhood. A person feels within himself a great release from the shackles of egocentricity. The other person is now seen through the eyes of unilateral love, a vision that transcends the petty dimensions of man's reciprocal love.

God loved us long before we even knew Him. In that curious logic of His, He loved us in spite of our weaknesses and colossal ingratitude. God did not love Peter any less after Peter had openly denied Him three times. He loved him more because that very act of denial and ingratitude only emphasized further the inadequacy of Peter's love and the need for an even further extension of God's love. (*See* John 13:36–38.)

Two people in mid-life, after the shambles of twenty or thirty years of a marriage that is a total travesty, finally look at one another. What each sees in the other person are all of the things that that person did to make the unhappy, unfulfilled person he is today. What each is saying is that if it were not for you and your emasculation or defeminization or coldness or greed or ambition or whatever, I would have been a happy, fulfilled person today. You, in effect, have ruined my life. What they might hopefully see is that it takes two to tango and that one person cannot do anything about the other person's contribution to the dance, but can only be responsible for his or her own actions. Each person should do all he can to change his attitudes and his contribution to the marriage, because marriage is something very important to hang on to, not only for each participant but for the children as well. This is the objective attitude any self-respecting psychiatrist would urge upon both partners in the marriage problem. It is, however, almost impossible to sell this idea to either one of the participants. There have been too many hurts. The process of rationalization has been working over too long a period of time without any counterbalance of objective logic.

That is why I believe that a Power that is beyond human power is needed to successfully regenerate a broken marriage at any stage, but especially in middle age when the pernicious patterns of mutual devitalization have been working for such a long period of time. Without the regenerative powers of the Holy Spirit the power of human understanding is not enough to unify that which has been smashed into a thousand pieces. With the position of Christ at the apex of each person's value system, a couple begins to see one another from the prospective of divine love. They gain that unilateral love that requires of the other person only the condition that he be available to love. It is love that searches out the good no matter how microscopic it might seem to be; a love that forgets the pettiness of the past; one that makes the person be willing and eager to deny himself for the other person. With this understanding of God's love, a person is not afraid to say, "I love you," and mean it, because the strength of that love is built not on the frail framework of human love but on the eternal strength of God's love operating with all of its eternal strength through a willing human being.

It is only when God's love is working through two people that marriage can reach the special kind of richness that is possible in middle life. For in middle life, we are dealing with people, who through the maturing process of human experience, have overcome the restless striving of youth that does not yet realize the limitations of its powers. They are people who have won and lost in their lives and not been destroyed by either, people who are free from their primary narcissism and can be sensitive to the needs of others—not as an extension of their own ego but as fellow human beings with similar dreams and disappointments.

It is the mature, middle-age person who, through understanding, can bring comfort to the lives of sons and daughters caught up in the storms of youth. This happens not so much by words as by the example of mature love based upon mutual understandings, self restraint, wisdom, and deep concern for the other person. This kind of example says something more meaningful than a thousand of the best-chosen words.

The greatest of all pleasures of married people in middle life is in the personal experiences they have shared. For those who have children there is the miracle of the coming of those tiny creatures who seem to be curious mixtures of both parents. There follows the development of those, at first, totally dependent organisms into unique independent human beings. The parents shared the careful steering of the offspring through the shoals of adolescence and the painful, but careful, release of loving restraint to assure a realistic sense of independence within the growing person. There were the concerns about vocation and marital goals; an increasing need of God's direction in all of these decisions; and, above all, the growing trust of one another. They experienced the opening of secret chambers of the self to effect a mutual trust and understanding. They grew to accept the fact that there may be certain areas of one's life that can never be shared; to accept imperfections as part of humanity in one's self and in one's partner. The growing intimacy of those middle years far surpassed in intensity that physical intimacy of the early years. There was the awareness of the clear manifestation of Christ-like characteristics in each person and evidence of that growing sense of oneness that is captured in the Scriptures' mysterious assertion that "they shall become one flesh." (*See* Genesis 2:24.)

7
LOVE: A Four-Letter Word

I asked her why she felt she had to leave her husband and four children. She looked me coolly in the eye and said, with very little change of expression, "Because I'm in love with another man." I hesitated, somewhat taken aback by the completeness of her composure, and then I continued with what seemed to me a perfectly logical question. "What do you mean by being in love?" She looked through me as though I were not there. She could not conceive of anyone being stupid enough to ask a question with such an obvious answer. She never gave me an answer, for the simple reason that she had no idea what love means.

Here was a young woman, at a crucial point in mid-life, ready to sacrifice her children, her husband, and the other man's family, all because she was driven by a process she could not even define. Not only that, but she felt perfectly justified in what she was doing because, "Love conquers all."

About a year ago a man in his mid-forties came into my office with a similar dilemma. He was a very successful man and a nice guy if I ever saw one. His problem was that he was in love with a young lady who was not his wife. His wife was a wonderful person, and like the nice guy that he was, he made no attempt to describe her as a dragon, as so many men do in similar situations. He had finally come to that difficult point of decision where he had to make up his mind whether to continue with his family or to set out into the sunset hand-in-hand with his true love. As a result, wife and family would have to go because, when true love comes along, you just cannot let it go by. This man was not any more successful in handling the question about love than the previously described young woman. I began to think of the thousands of people who, every year, find themselves in similar situations, ready to sacrifice everything on the altar of love when they have no idea of what love is all about. What is this curious emotion that is so powerful that it cuts across all lines of reason and propriety? No one can deny its preoccupation in the minds of human beings. It is everywhere. Its magic adorns the theatre marquees along Broadway and nestles in the dancing lights of Forty-Second Street. You observe it etched on plastic bracelets and iron rings on counters in dime stores, embroidered on tapestries in elegant drawing rooms, scribbled with chalk on subway walls, tattooed on hairy forearms, painted on the sides of Volkswagen buses, or printed in big red letters on the fronts of white T-shirts. The hippy cult is enamored with the concept and pours out its praises in soft, cool monosyllables. Any psychiatrist worth his salt will tell you that most of the emotional illnesses today would be nonexistent if the victims had known something of love. Kids would not be freaking out on drugs. Marriages would not be breaking up. There would be no murders, robberies, war, or violence if the people would just learn to love. Yet everyone who has been around this planet long enough knows that people, supposedly motivated by love, have committed crimes of violence exceedingly vicious and cruel, the kinds of actions that supposedly disappear if one does things under the influence of love.

What then is the answer to this curious paradox? Can love be defined? Does it mean anything? Most people agree that love is a feeling, and few deny that it is a pleasant one. It is an absorbing emotion and, when active, dominates all other mental faculties. It is magnetic and draws loved ones together. Ideally it is concerned with the well-being of the other person, and yet the popular variety of lover is often jealous, possessive, and basically egocentric. There is love that is considerate, yet often it lacks consideration. People in love really do not care that much about anyone or anything else, but real love, it is said, is selfless. It involves sacrifice and responsibility. And so we dip into the pool of the meaning of love and come up with many strange and different fish, none of which give us any direct meaning of the word itself. Perhaps it is a process that transcends definition, like so many other important concepts of human life, but love is a concept of such towering importance that it demands serious contemplation.

The first contact human beings have with love is through their mothers. It began when they were still in the aqueous phase of human development. What mothers thought of them even before they were born affected their well-being. If the mothers looked forward to their advents with anxiety or ambivalence, that feeling was transmitted into their vascular systems through hormones. They felt that fear and rejection. It made a mark on their inactive minds and, because of that, the process of love beyond the uterus was hampered. On the other hand, if the mothers looked forward to their coming with joy, that exhilarating feeling reflected itself in the offsprings' natures and the process of love outside the uterus went on unimpeded. Love was the important message in those first few years of prenatal life. How important it was to know that somebody cared! There was no way of taking care of oneself; at that stage of the game a person could not even feed himself, let alone speak the language. He was helpless and, to a certain extent, lost. He needed encouragement to go on in this brave new world that he never asked to be put into. Most mothers have little trouble giving the kind of love and attention that these tiny creatures need.

One of the first requirements in the process of development of any normal personality is that of self-acceptance. That acceptance comes through the mother. Her love shows the infant that

his existence is worthwhile. That love, although totally acceptable to the infant in those early days, gradually is shaped by the
fact that many of the impulses that drive the infant into action
need discipline. If baby does everything he wants, then he is
totally under the tyranny of his instincts. His world becomes a
choiceless one because he can make no decisions contrary to the
direction of his instincts. Here then we see that a mother's love
cannot be without discrimination. It must bear the mark of discipline for, without it, the child would never be able to love anybody
but himself.

On the other hand, if he gets no love at all, he will never love
anybody, not even himself. Without a healthy self-love a person
can never really love any other person. Did not the Lord say,
"Love thy neighbor as thyself"? (*See* Mark 12:33.) That love
then comes first from the mother. It is a love that accepts one for
what he is. It is delighted in the child's preferences and seeks out
and encourages his talents. It uncovers his limitations and teaches
him to accept them. Out of this kind of relationship comes a
human being who can love.

Too often we see the opposite—a person who is loved not for
what he is, but for what he can do. Such a person can never really
accept himself because he is afraid that what he really is, is not
good enough. And so, he attempts to do something else. His goals
never come from within, but always from without. Life is a drama
and he is the actor. Basically such people are dishonest. They
never see themselves as they really are, but only as other people
want them to be. The real person is lost in the shuffle of life and
can never really love because love is something he never let himself experience.

There are still other people, people who never know anything
of love at all. They are totally rejected as infants. They are un-
wanted to begin with, and everything they do is unacceptable.
Self-acceptance is never possible for these unfortunates. The continual message received is rejection. At some time in their tiny,

developing minds, they come to the conclusion that "if you can't beat them, then join them." They begin to hate themselves and, in effect, they join the other team where at least they feel on somebody's side. Their lives from now on are dedicated to failure. They become connoisseurs of the negative, virtuosos of despair. Their capacity to love is zero. Mother's love—or lack of it—leaves a mark, shapes the templet that determines the capacity of her infant to love and be loved.

One day the child's attention moves away from himself and his mother, and he discovers a world of objects and people beyond himself. To be sure, at first, they are simply extensions of himself, but, in time, he lets go of this delusion and sees them as autonomous figures. His love is extended to the things that give him pleasure. He loves the rattle because, when he shakes it, it makes a noise. It gives him a sense of power and control. Possession gives him pleasure, but loss of possession, displeasure. He must learn that he cannot have everything he wants. Some things belong to other people and he must respect that. If he belongs to that group whose primary love was never satisfied, he keeps reaching out for more and more. To him nothing ever belongs to anybody else, only himself. He can never let go of self. The objects only have value to the extent that they can give pleasure to him or inflate his ego.

This period of development adds its own ingredients to the process of love for it produces two general categories of people—one group cannot stand looking at themselves and the others cannot stop. The ones who cannot look at themselves are the ones who were never looked at, or were looked at only with displeasure. They are the ones who were rejected by their mothers. They move away from any situation that would bring attention to themselves. Of course, they do not see that in doing so they are continually aware of themselves. They are involved in the process of negative narcissism, fascinated by their own worthlessness. Their life becomes a game of "I dare you to show me that I'm worthwhile in any way." No matter what one says or does, they can never change that deeply based conviction of worthlessness. They are all wrapped up in themselves negatively. Only occasionally do they emerge from this cocoon of despair, and then they appear for a fascinating moment only to quickly scurry back into the darkened corners, spinning their own webs of despair, waiting for some Prince Charming to cut away the brambles and wake the sleeping princess. "All we want is love," they say, "or the opportunity to love somebody else," but the longer they wait, the more impossible becomes their goal.

Another group never gets much involved with things outside themselves because they never stop looking at themselves. Get them in a room with a mirror and they jockey around until they get in their special spot—right in front of the mirror. They talk to you, but they are only watching themselves. They tilt their heads to a more charming angle, move into the softer shadows that bring out more delicate contours of their faces, leave their mouths open just a fraction of a second longer to show their perfectly aligned teeth. They never listen, they just wait for you to stop talking. Their game becomes "love me because I'm lovable." Their big mission in life is to sign up as many volunteers for their own love-me brigade as possible. So they turn their charms on this one and that one hoping for as many admirers as possible. Their moves are studied, their techniques catching. It is almost impossible to resist them, that is, until their game becomes clear and it is obvious there is nothing there because they only see themselves. It never occurs to them that, no matter how hard they look they can never really see themselves. We were made to look at other people. God knew what He was doing when he built us that way. In spite of this anatomical advantage, people spend their lives using every possible psychological contortion to get a better glimpse of that gorgeous sight—themselves. So quite early in life, the stage is set for the struggle between self-love and the love of things other than self. The person who has been truly loved does not need to be in love with himself. He is able to accept himself as he really is, for the person who has loved him has done so in a true sense. He has loved him for what he is. The person who loves himself in a healthy way is able to forget himself, but the person who is continually conscious of himself can never really love himself.

At some particular point in time, a new factor enters the cauldron of developing love. Love for Mother was a subtle way of extending the closeness that existed *in utero*. It made the passage into the new world a little more enjoyable. Now it allows us to accept our essential state of aloneness. A person who finds himself a good companion does not really *need* anybody else. This puts him in the position of *wanting* someone else, which is a lot healthier and honest than needing. One is obliged to be grateful to the person he needs, but he can love the person he wants with no strings attached. The new factor that is added to the process of love is sex.

Now sex adds to love an element that is both pleasing and disturbing. Few are aware of its first appearance because it has so many subtle ways of generating. At some particular point in time, a person begins to engage in sexual fantasies. This can be as innocent as wanting to hold the hand of the little girl who lives down the street. It is a thought that is hard to shake because it is so delightful. He finds himself carrying it with him wherever he goes. He may never even speak to the child, but she is his constant companion. Along the pathways of imagination most people have had many such delightful companions, now lodged in the forgotten compartments of their minds. The element of sex adds a factor of delight, but also one of obsession because it becomes very difficult for one to dislodge the object of that desire from one's mind. There can be little doubt that the whole process of sexual attraction is linked with the unconscious desire to return to the bliss of the uterus. There is a compulsive drive to touch and hold, to become a part of the warmth and intimacy of the loved object. Sexual drives are essentially egocentric. The love object is a focal point of attention, but the real pleasure is the one that occurs within the individual participant. The sexual factor in love is a loaded one. Although it increases the intensity of the love process, it also adds ego gratification which is essentially a centripetal action. It is also indiscriminate in its most basic form, even though it seems specific at the particular time of involvement. Such factors dictate the necessity of responsibility and control. Without these elements, sex can change the love process into one of ravage and exploitation. The intensity of the sexual drive, as part of the process of love, can be very misleading.

In our day and time, love has become synonymous with sexual love. The ultimate variety is seen as two people become totally involved with one another on every level of existence, so totally absorbed with one another that they forget everything and everybody else in the world. They clutch one another like two little embryos swimming through the amniotic fluid, joined in a physical and psychological symbiosis that finds its most idyllic expression in Hollywood movie scripts. The duration of such a relationship in terms of reality is, at best, very brief. Such total mutual absorption is only possible *in utero*. The entrance of the sexual theme into the symphony of love intensifies the process but also introduces the necessity for control and responsibility, and exposes the person to a mechanism that is both egocentric and regressive.

At some time in man's experience, he is confronted with God's love. I do not mean the kind of love spoken of by people who intimate that God *is* human love. Such a concept reduces God to a feeling or a vague repository of divine nectar that makes people drool over one another. God's love is a deeply personal process between two people—the individual and God. "For God so loved the world, that he gave his only begotten Son, that whosoever believeth in him should not perish, but have everlasting life."

(John 3:16.) God's love, then, is not a feeling but a giving. What He gave was more than a dozen roses—He gave His own Son. He did not give Him for just a few hours to help us with some of our problems. He gave His Son to die for us. Now from a human point of view, one might well ask, "What kind of a morbid God is this who would sacrifice His Son to die for anyone, especially for people who showed God so little love themselves but rather, only a cold, arrogant rejection?" The questioner might well add, "I would never give my son to die for anyone. I love him too much. I'd destroy anybody who laid a finger on him." The paradoxical thing about God's love is that because of His love for His Son, he permitted Him to die. For God knew that that love would spawn a new breed of human beings, free of the primary narcissism of self-love, free to worship God in the way that God wanted to be worshipped, able to share in that love bond that existed between the Father and the Son; and able to demonstrate in their lives a quality of love that is both selfless and giving.

Divine love then is unilateral. It is offered in spite of what one is or does. It is love characterized by sacrifice, pain, deprivation, and selflessness. That is the only kind of love that can fill the craters left by the deprivations of childhood. No earthly love can ever fill the needs inherent in that kind of love. It also is the only kind of love that can remove the contaminants of regression, possessiveness, and egocentricity inherent in the other kinds of love.

We see then that love appears in many forms and under many guises, but there is only one *real* love in human experience. That is the mature love that God speaks of in His Word. It is the love described in the thirteenth chapter of First Corinthians. It is a love that includes all of the good things and excludes the bad. It is the kind of love that can change the world, but will never be found blazing in the lights of Broadway or heard in the mystical rhythms of rock music. In its depth and beauty, it exceeds the loftiest dreams of man. This kind of love first suffereth long and is kind. (*See* 1 Corinthians 13:4.) That is, it looks for a way of being constructive and it is slow to lose patience.

Young woman, staring at me with your cold, gray eyes, do you know anything of this kind of love? How patient were you with the one you no longer love? Can you see beyond your petulance the tragedy of his life that was swept up in the angry swirl of corporate business? Can you see beyond your own immaturity and egocentricity? Did you let go of your childish fantasies? How constructive did you really try to be? Right love also envieth not: that is, it is not possessive. Oh, I realize you cannot see a speck of your wanting to be possessive of your husband. In fact, you would like to get rid of him, but what about your new love? Are you sure your proposed plan is really best for his life situation? Do you recognize the intensity of it all? You have never felt like this about anyone—well, not since you left the uterus anyway. That same love vaunteth not itself, is not puffed up. (*See* verse 4.) That is, it is neither anxious to impress nor does it cherish inflated ideas of its own importance.

Yes, I know you are a nice guy, a forty-seven-year-old man, ready to chuck your family for this cute, young secretary with the long, blond hair. I will bet somebody like that would not have given you the time of day when you were her age, would she? Remember you were a skinny kind of kid then, with a pimply face. Well, you are more impressive now with your prosperous figure and the longish hair, graying at the temples. The expensive suit does not hurt you much, either. But most of all it is the nice-guy role that is impressive. Do you know what Leo Durocher, the baseball player, said about nice guys? "Okay, they lose ball games, but they win hearts." Is that it? We know you do not think you are important, but you think you are nice. Well, I have news for you. You may be neither, but you are more important than you are nice. And it also says in God's Word that love does not behave itself unseemly. (*See* verse 5.) That is, it has good manners. It has self-control. It does not hurt people just because it wants something that will make it feel good. It does not sacrifice human beings to pay tribute to the goddess of beauty.

Oh, yes, distressed young lady, you feel great, snuggled up to your new love. You will be the sleeping princess and he will be the prince charming, but what about the poor little confused children staring into the darkness of the night? What is really going through their minds? Are they wondering where Daddy is tonight, or what that strange man is doing in Mommy's room?

And, of course, love seeketh not its own. That is, it is not egotistical. Oh, you are not egotistical, I know. It is just that you want to give everything to her, is not that so? You do not have a selfish bone in your body when it comes to her, do you? Would it not be great to be seen with somebody like that, walking along the shore in Bermuda? Everybody on the beach would envy you, would they not? How about those dinners at night under the tropical moon with her in a low-cut gown and you in your white dress suit? And then, after that, you'll be walking barefoot through the waters that lap along the shore. That is kind of an ego-trip, is it not?

Love is not easily provoked. That is, it is not touchy. But you seem pretty touchy to me, especially when I direct the conversation to subjects like responsibility. They seem pretty corny, do they not? You want to talk of more profound things—the majesty and beauty of love—except that you were never able to define it, were you?

Love thinketh no evil and rejoices not in iniquity, but rejoices in the truth. (*See* verse 6.) That is, love does not keep an account of evil or gloat over the wickedness of other people. It seems to me that you had a veritable catalog of all the things your husband did that were wrong. Right, you do not love him, but what makes you think a new catalog of shortcomings will not build up with your new friend? Oh, yes, I forgot you are "in love." But he is a human being, is he not? He will make mistakes. In speaking of the truth, how honest have you been about this whole situation? Oh, yes, I know all about his wrongs, but what about your contribution? It takes two to tango, you know. Did you really try to right all of the wrongs that you did, or did you just sit like a cat ready to pounce on a mouse whenever he made another mistake? Love bears all things. (*See* verse 7.) That is to say, there is no limit to its endurance. I know you gave your all. He was cruel and insensitive, totally egocentric. And I know you will follow your new love to the dark side of the moon. It is just that your track record on this planet has not been so hot. If I had to make a bet, I would not make book on your chances over the long run, in your new relationship, either.

The thirteenth chapter of First Corinthians also says that, love believeth all things, hopeth all things, endureth all things. Yes, I am sure you will always trust her, even six months from now when you are on the ski slopes in Switzerland and some young Austrian ski instructor helps her tie her boot, which somehow came loose at that particular time. You notice what a handsome couple they make as the sun beats down on their tan, young faces. Suddenly you feel old and very much like her father. Then off they go, whisking down the mountainside, and you wish you had stayed home by the fire, where it was warm, and read a book. I am sure your hope will never die. It had better not. You paid a high price for it. What about that hope that you had twenty-three years ago? What happened to that one? I guess hopes are easy to hold onto when you are really in love, but in twenty-three more years you will be seventy and it will not make much difference then, will it? Maybe love can outlast everything but life. Is that it? I would not deny the intensity and the magnetism of your kind of relationship, but it has no staying power. Its tolerances are too narrow, its duration too brief. The next time this kind of thing happens to you do not say you are in love, say you are involved. You are caught up in a narcissistic ego-trip that really does not care about anything but itself.

The two people we have been discussing have been caught up in a mid-life crisis of love. They made commitments before an altar and an audience many years ago, but somehow they have forgotten them. Their present love, in spite of its intensity, lacks commitment because they are in no position to make such a transaction. Theirs is a neurotic love. They are hung up on themselves, involved with infantile fixations. In running away from reality and responsibility, they are up to their necks in something exciting and intriguing, but, of one thing you can be sure, they are not in love.

We see then that love is a multifaceted process. It begins in the mother's womb before the fetus is aware that there is a world outside. The process continues with the wordless years of infancy and on into the various stages of human development. We see the mother as the all-important figure in the development of that love. We notice that love is something that begins as an egocentric mechanism then gradually moves out towards other things and other people. Too often the magnetic pull of egocentricity is so great that it stunts the growth of the love forces that might be directed to things other than self. We have observed the way sexual drives add another dimension to love. To some people this physical-love component becomes the overpowering factor in any love relationship. It is indeed a sad thing that so many human beings can only relate intimately to another person on a physical level no loftier than the beasts of the field. The full expression of love contains all of the elements of man's existence, not only physical but also mental and spiritual. The mental aspects of love not only contain feelings, but even more importantly, understanding, sensitivity to the needs of the other person, and self-control, which, in many instances, may mean setting aside one's own desires to support another person. It is that selflessness that is so difficult to attain when one lives life on the basis of a two-dimensional model, that is, physical and mental. In the two-dimensional life process, the physical component is often the dominating one, and, certainly, in the popular philosophy of our day, the only one. The sexual component of physical love should be the least important part of a relationship. It is, of course, the most primitive one. Its function is bound up with urges that are rooted in the most basic of biological mechanisms, that is, the reflex. Choice, that human function which distinguishes us from nonhuman creatures, is not involved in reflex activity. When the stud horse, grazing in the field, notices a mare in the next field, the force that causes him to jump the fence has nothing to do with choice, but everything to do with instinctual compulsion. Yet it is this reflex compulsion that is at the nucleus of most people's concept of love.

What people are able to ignore with the easiest facility is the spiritual image of love. If there is a God, then the basis of complete love would have to place God's love at the apex of that love process. God has a special love for human beings. He arranged for us to have accessible the greatest love relationship possible for any living creature. We, with all of our human frailties, with our inability to measure up to God's standards in even the slightest way, are given the opportunity to be His children if we accept His Son as our Saviour. By that acceptance, we can call God "our Father" in a claim that goes far beyond that of our earthly fathers, who, in spite of their love, are, nevertheless, checkered with the inadequacies of human nature. The principle of God's love, as we mentioned before, is that it is unilateral. God loves us in spite of our failures, rather than because of our virtues.

It is in the shadows of mid-life that man's mind begins to mellow so that he can enter into the full participation of real love. The concept of mature love does not reject the physical component of love but is able to see its self-limiting capacity and is able to enjoy the control of this powerful urge rather than be bondsman to its unpredictable forces. This kind of love incorporates understanding and wisdom, the ability to be sensitive to the needs of other people, and the capacity to put that sensitivity into useful action. Mature love embraces an expression of the full range of human emotions and has the ability never to deny the emotion but to control that emotion, if its expression will hurt some other person. In addition, we think of the other qualities of mature love— its patience, its freedom from self, its sense of responsibility, its constructiveness and humility, its self-control, fairness, and desire for the truth, its endurance, trust, and hope, its durability, its capacity to remain stable when everything else has failed, and, that most important ingredient of all, its commitment. One really cannot love someone unless he has made a commitment to that person. Without commitment, love has no adhesiveness. Without commitment, the integrity of love is based upon physical instinct, which is too unreliable. Above all, the concept of complete love must reflect God's love, so that it will contain that unilateral quality free of self-seeking motivation so prevalent in human love. This is a love that enables us to reach out beyond the realms of self-interest into the lives of other people. It is a love that gives to its possessor a sense of security and peace, which goes far beyond human understanding. It is a love that causes its possessor to say with the Apostle Paul, "For I am persuaded, that neither death, nor life, nor angels, nor principalities, nor powers, nor things present, nor things to come, nor height, nor depth, nor any other creature, shall be able to separate us from the love of God, which is in Christ Jesus our Lord." (Romans 8:38, 39.) The pervasiveness of that dimension of love reinforces all of the other components of the concept and draws them together into a cohesive whole, which provides the ultimate model of love in human experience. It is this love that all Christians have access to, no matter where they are in their journey up the mountain of life; however, it is in mid-life that this love should begin to show itself more clearly in the lives of those who call themselves Christians.

8

The Golden Years of Christian Maturity

It is in mid-life that the Christian has the greatest opportunity to demonstrate the truth of what he believes. The unrealistic idealism of youth has yielded to the harshness of reality, making it quite clear that life is not an unending bed of roses or an unbroken chain of joy. In spite of the best laid plans of mice and men, unpleasant accidents intrude upon our experience. Dreams he counted on are never materialized, and human beings whom he trusted so deeply have let him down. Perhaps the greatest disappointment of all occurs within himself. In middle age, unpleasant aspects of his own personality begin to emerge—perhaps a hidden pettiness, a tendency to be overly critical, or even to play the fool in certain circumstances. He may shy away from these unpleasant traits that begin to show through the veneer of his posture. The threat of truth about himself may be so great that he builds higher and higher barriers of denial and distorts his personality even more. The real threat of self-realization is the fear that one cannot teach an old dog new tricks. If there is never a need for new tricks, the dog will never have to demonstrate his inadequacy. That is why so many middle-aged people find so much security in the accustomed routines of their lives. They view this time of life as a holding pattern. For many human beings, especially businessmen, this is the zenith of their careers. The shape of their achievement has been clearly defined. They will have to be satisfied with fixed limits of their potential. From here on in, they will have to coast. Retirement, the ultimate dream of younger years, begins to cast its shadow across the life of middle-aged people.

As we mentioned before, the character of mid-life is such that it forces the mind to consider the transitory quality of man's existence. It is an age that demands, in so many ways, the need for man to consider the spiritual side of his existence. He begins to see the shortcomings of trusting in other physical or mental things for his security. He begins to be able to face the grim significance of David's statement in Psalms 103:15, 16, "As for man, his days are as grass: as a flower of the field, so he flourisheth. For the wind passeth over it, and it is gone; and the place thereof shall know it no more." It is when man is in middle age, halfway up the mountain, that he begins to sense that fleeting, elusive part of his nature that intrudes itself into his life more emphatically with the passage of each day. Most people suppress this troubling aspect of their nature. To think about it even a little bit fills them with disquieting thoughts that are too painful to consider. They live for the moment, for that is all they think that they have, and they do not have that for very long. "Eat, drink, and be merry, for tomorrow we die." What consolation is there in logic as they consider the briefness of their own existence? Psalm Ninety declares, "Man's life is like a tale told." (*See* verse 9.) Shakespeare embellished it with the thought that man's life is not just a tale told, but "Told by an idiot, full of sound and fury, signifying nothing." These are the words of a beleaguered Macbeth, but they represent the logical end point of man's consideration of life from the perspective of finite logic.

Because of our faith, we Christians are free of the restricting bonds of reason. God's Word makes it very clear that man's destiny transcends the tiny interval of earth time. As earth creatures, our conscious experience is but the beginning of a destiny which goes beyond our finite natures. In John 14:2, 3, the Lord makes it quite clear that, "I go to prepare a place for you. . . . that where I am, there ye may be also." The uniqueness of the Christian experience that distinguishes it so clearly from the non-Christian is that the Christian not only has an awareness of his finite experience but, through the power of the Holy Spirit, he has a special consciousness of his infinite dimension as well. Men generally tend to live in a two-dimensional life. Life to them is lived within the perimeters of their physical and mental experiences. To go beyond that, as Freud once stated, is to tread in the "black mud of occultism." The belief that the spiritual dimension of man's nature will not oblige a scientific model is, for many scientists, good enough reason to put it in the same category as madness. In the scientific world seeing is believing and this attitude is absolutely necessary for objective physical and mental investigation. Furthermore, that seeing, or physical manifestation, must be repeatable in similar, but different, situations. The very basis of spiritual life is that believing is seeing. To believe in Christ is to receive a new means of perception. Faith is a very confusing concept to the world. In fact, it makes no sense at all. To the world it is the Christian's greatest weakness. To the Christian it is his greatest strength.

In mid-life, the Christian faith should be showing signs of maturity. The basic faith the Christian has is in his belief in the Lord Jesus Christ as his personal Saviour. That was the faith that turned on the lights of the new world, but there is nothing static about that faith. The meaning of Christ's death for the Christian should grow in all of its dimensions as he grows more mature as a Christian. Because as the meaning becomes clearer to him, he begins to be more aware of Christ as a Person, and the more real He becomes as a Person, the more the Christian will identify with Him in his life. He will then become not an imitator of Christ, but rather one who *emits* Christ. He will grow with His love not because he, in some inferior way, tried to imitate Him, but because of an unconscious process beyond his control that compels his person to radiate in His love and power.

How many Christians do you know whose life glows in this arresting fashion? These are Christians who even the world finds fascinating, not by the drabness of their dress nor their apparent immunity to anything of a cultural nature, nor by their sometimes flamboyant display of negative behavior—they don't drink, smoke, go to movies—but because of their stability, their capacity to maintain composure in situations where most people would crumble in despair, their ability to go into any negative situation and identify and work with the positive elements. On the other hand, it is one of the saddest commentaries on Christianity that the only outstanding thing about some Christians' lives seems to be a penchant for negative behavior.

When a Christian moves into and through middle life, his life should begin to take on a mark of maturity that is instantly recognizable. The Christian life should be characterized by wisdom. Wisdom is not something that is the product of any curriculum. There are many people who have abundant knowledge, but are almost imbecilic in their use of that knowledge. In Proverbs 1:7, we are told, "The fear of the Lord is the beginning of knowledge." Without that focal point then, one cannot even begin to be wise. The mark of a truly wise man is that he fears or is aware of God's presence at all times. In a world that clamors for attention in a thousand ways, it is not always easy to be aware of God. The Lord does not flash brilliant lights at us, or cause bells to ring in our ears. The one thing that augments that *fear* more than any other is the knowledge of God's Word. For although the world is full of the manifestations of His creative power, both at microscopic and macroscopic levels, it is in God's Word only that we learn about God's personality. Many knowledgeable men see God as some supreme creative force, but they hesitate to describe His personality or even to concede that God is a Person. That, of course, is because they have known Him only as a power and turn their backs on the only document that reveals God's Person. But more of that later.

So Christians in mid-life should begin to manifest God's wisdom in their lives. They should be known as men and women who will listen and listen in such a way as to increase learning. Many men find it difficult to listen at all. They simply wait for the other person to stop talking. They do not want to hear what you have to say. By the blank look in their eyes, you get the uncomfortable feeling that you are boring them. When you talk to a wise man, you are immediately aware that he is listening carefully to everything you say. He listens not to criticize, not to defend his own position, but to learn. To have that kind of wisdom is a very exciting thing. It is again, the kind of thing that becomes more easily accessible in middle life with its moderating effects upon the human psyche.

I wonder how many middle-aged Christians are respected for their wisdom. I am afraid too often what happens is that they are known more for their closed minds, their rigidity, their legalism. They are not the first, but the very last people whom a person in trouble would go to with a problem. The difficulty is that so many of them equate Christianity with a life without problems. What they seem to imply is that if you have problems, it is because you are not a good Christian. But was not our Lord a Person who was familiar with problems? Did not the prophet Isaiah describe him as "a man of sorrows, and acquainted with grief?" (*See* Isaiah 53:3.) Should not then the maturing Christian have a sympathetic sensitivity to the problems that far surpass the empathy of those who have never been touched with God's love in a personal way? Should he not be ready to get involved with the resolution of those problems as someone who is motivated by love rather than by a desire to inflate his own ego? The Christian, who becomes involved with other people's problems, should never do so from the point of view, "You've got problems and I don't," which is obviously a vertical position of superiority, but rather, "You've got problems and I empathize with this because I've been there myself." The mark of a wise person is his ability to identify with the problem not to just leave it there in mutual surrender to it, but to help, knowing the solution to any person's problem lies within the person himself. We can never work out other people's salvation or lives for them. The Lord very implicitly indicates that we should "work out our own salvation with fear and trembling." (*See* Philippians 2:12.)

It is perhaps in this one area that so many immature Christians fail in their dealings with other people. We must never limit the power of the Holy Spirit, but we must recognize that this human being is finite. We have specific limitations in our own ability to help other people. If we overhelp, we deprive them of the only chance they have for real help, which, of course, is that help which comes from mobilizing the strengths that they have within themselves. We can encourage them to identify and use that strength, but we can never supply or be the strength. To do so would make us thieves.

The Christian then should be known as a person who always respects the dignity of the other human being. Who, even though he knows the truth, is neither superior in his attitude to the other person, who is ignorant of the truth, nor intimidated by the person who rejects the truth. How easy it is to actively reject or gradually become indifferent to the person who rejects the Gospel. What a tragedy it would have been for us if that person who led us to Christ had become either indifferent, superior, or embarrassed. I do not believe that we should badger a person with an endless chant of John 3:16. That would be the very antithesis of wisdom, but we, as mid-life Christians who know the shocking brevity of life, should never overlook the fact that God brings us into contact with people for reasons that go far beyond the apparent meaning of that encounter. God's love extends to every living soul. For the mature mid-life Christian knows that nothing happens casually in his life (*see* Romans 8:28). Christians do not have chance encounters with anyone. It is all part of God's never-ending work to reach every man with the Gospel. But our attitudes should not reflect the mind of the hunter who has set his snare for the rabbit, or the fisherman who has baited his hook for the fish. There should be no sense of the predator in any of our actions. We are indeed to be fishers of men, but only in the sense that we are instruments to be used and directed by the Holy Spirit. The awareness of the Spirit's activity in our lives provides the proper attitude that will allow us not only to be spectators of God's unending work of grace, but also, to become an active, integral part of the elaboration of that work as well.

The mid-life-Christian's prayer should not be something that he ought to do. It should be something that he cannot do without. The Lord said, in Luke 18:1 "Men ought always to pray and not to faint." And Paul said we should pray without ceasing. (*See* 1 Thessalonians 5:17.) Prayer is our verbal connection with God. It makes us aware of His presence and alerts us to our dependency upon him. Without the perspective that prayer gives us we can too easily go off in our own egocentric ways and sabotage God's plan for us. By mid-life a person should be able to look back on his experience and recognize the specific way in which God has guided his life. Too often we can recite all we have done for Him, but have little recall of how much He has done for us. It is prayer that brings us back to that special awareness of God's hand in our lives.

Many people of the world are scornful of prayer. They see it as a regression into infantile dependency. Why should the mature person not be master of his own fate? Why should he get involved with a mild form of delusional thinking because he does not have the courage to stand on his own two feet? These kinds of thoughts come from minds that oversimplify the whole process of human life. This whole attitude stems from an arrogancy that is born of ignorance. If we knew even a fraction of the forces that come to bear upon our lives, not only in the external environment but the internal as well, we would be in constant prayer for God's guidance, and help, and protection. Too often our prayers are token prayers, mindless generalities spoken to appease a God who is not too particular and to placate our own consciences. We may, in a vague way, feel that to be a good Christian we ought to let God in on our act some way.

What the middle-aged Christian should be aware of is the capacity of prayer to change things or get things done. This power is the Christian's greatest source of spiritual energy. How tragic that halfway up the mountain so few Christians have known anything about that kind of power. They do not use prayer in their daily lives because they rationalize that God could not possibly be interested in all the petty little details of their existence. How wrong they are! It is out of the tiny increments of existence that a life is built. If you only have God involved in the crises of your life, you are going to exclude Him almost altogether. God wants crisis time, but He also wants time in the broad hiatus between the crises. When the character of our relationship with Him is less on the basis of urgency and more on the basis of continual fellowship, our lives will reflect that peace of God that passes human understanding. God's peace comes to the person who shares every aspect of his life with God. David not only knew God's peace when he lay beside the still waters and contemplated His shepherding love, but he knew that peace, perhaps even more emphatically, when he walked through the valley of the shadow of death and felt God's presence with him. David could say in the very midst of his enemies that "he feared no evil," because "thou art with me." The presence of the enemy was ominous, but David was more sensitive to God's presence and God's power. "Thy rod and thy staff, they comfort me." (*See* Psalms 23:4.) David sensed that power as clearly as if he held God's staff himself.

Prayer, of course, is based upon faith: faith that there is a personal God who hears; faith that the God who hears will also listen to our prayers; faith that He loves us as individuals and is, therefore, interested in every aspect of our lives; faith that God will not turn a deaf ear on those who cry out to Him.

The thing that puzzles many people about prayer is that it seems to be a one-way communication. There is only one voice involved. In times past, God not infrequently would communicate with man by His own voice. He may still do so in some instances, but none that I am familiar with. It is this one-way communication and this zone of silence that puzzles so many nonbelievers. "How can you talk with somebody who never answers you back?" they ask. It is not enough to tell them that God has already spoken His word in the Bible. They cannot really understand that. They might not understand any better the fact that God speaks to us in the things that happen to us in our daily lives—through the people we meet, the disappointments that occur, the successes we have, the unexpected surprises that occur so often. What is so difficult for them to understand is that God, through the Holy Spirit, speaks in the very words that we pray. For most people prayer is asking for something. We cannot deny that that is part of the function. Did not the Lord Himself encourage us to ask for things when He told His disciples, "Whatsoever ye shall ask in my name, that will I do, that the Father may be glorified in the Son." (John 14:13.) The Lord encourages us to ask because the answering of our requests is not only one of His greatest avenues of personal revelation, but also a way in which He buttresses our often floundering faith.

As we mature in our Christian lives, we begin to learn that prayers are not only requests for God's hand in the trials of our lives, but for praises as well. Halfway up the mountain our prayers should be characterized more by praise of God for His love and His existence. The prayer of praise is an expression of love. It is in the prayer of praise that the Holy Spirit is more evidently in charge. Prayers for requests are finally focused on the problem itself. We are asking God to help us in a specific situation, whether it be help for a sick friend or guidance in an important life decision. The main motivating mechanism in such prayer is need. The character of that prayer, then, is built according to the templet of the need.

We can see that prayers of request for personal need have a conspicuous element of egocentricity. On the other hand, prayers of praise are free of any egocentricity, for their focal point is God Himself. The Holy Spirit is able to work with the freer hand in this kind of prayer, for praise of God has no boundary lines. In fact, praise of God from an intellectual base, runs aground very quickly. It is when the Holy Spirit takes over, that the prayer of praise takes on a transcendent quality that gives that prayer a special kind of beauty, and to the person who prays and to those who listen, an ecstatic sense of God's love and peace.

Another thing that determines the character of the mid-life Christian is his familiarity with God's Word and his ability to apply that Word to every aspect of his life. We all know people who seem to have an encyclopedic knowledge of God's Word. They can recite great reams of it at the drop of a hat. They also take great pride in being able to interpret certain passages with a virtuosolike flair. But as one looks at their personal lives, one sees that they are riddled with inconsistencies. The man who can spell out God's love so beautifully from Scripture often fails to give any indication that he knows anything of that love in terms of dealing with other human beings. The Lord makes it quite clear in Matthew 4:4, ". . . Man shall not live by bread alone, but by every word that proceedeth out of the mouth of God." It would almost seem that many people have the capacity of gathering great quantities of God's Word, but show no signs of eating it. They wear it like a badge, but give no indication that they have any intention of assimilating it. Unless God's Word is assimilated, it is nothing more than great literature. Our minds are enriched by great literature, but we can live without it. We cannot, however, live spiritually, as Christians, without God's Word. It is indeed the most powerful growth factor in the Christian's life. By mid-life the Christian should feel hungry when he does not have a significant portion of God's Word every day. It is interesting that we seldom miss a meal in our lives no matter how pressed we are for time. Even though we may have plenty of surplus energy in the fat depots of our bodies, we have appetites that force us to the table at certain times of the day. If, through some extreme situation, we cannot eat for three or four days, our bodies begin to take on an emaciated look and our energy falls to very low levels. Unfortunately, our spiritual beings do not reflect separation from spiritual food in such a dramatic way. We can go many days without turning to God's Word, and to all outward, and even inward, appearances show no signs of spiritual starvation. Spiritual starvation shows signs of its presence in insidious ways. Christ-centeredness is gradually replaced by egocentricity. In other words, man's priority system is subtly restructured. At the apex of the Christian's priority system is the person of the Lord Jesus Christ, but that is not a static system. Each day it is under the attack. Satan never ceases his work to undermine the positional ascendency of Christ in the Christian's life. Satan wants the ego in the dominant position of each Christian's life because if the ego is in a position of supremacy, Satan can turn his mind to other things. He knows the human ego, no matter how dignified, can only move in a downward spiral. It is incapable of resisting the negative pull of the vicious cycle of sin and death that we have mentioned elsewhere. As we discussed above, "The fear of the Lord is the beginning of wisdom." (*See* Psalms 11:10.) That fear or awe is something that must be rekindled every day.

The daily feeding from God's Word not only helps us to maintain the priority systems that are necessary for any kind of Christian activity, but also, through the wisdom and understanding that it provides, prepares us for spiritual experiences not possible for those Christians whose spiritual life is maintained on lesser diets.

So many Christians settle for lives that reflect, at best, the treading of water. They keep their heads above the surface to the extent that one can always identify them as Christians, but they are not moving anywhere. They are never free to reach out to any other person because they are too busy trying to keep their own heads above water. They never lose their identity, but they do lose their power. They lose the power available to them through the freedom that Christ has given them through His redemptive work.

It is that freedom which should begin to appear in the life of the mid-life Christian, a freedom that releases the Christian from the built-in egocentricity of his own psyche, a freedom that allows him to love and serve other people (*see* Galatians 5:13).

Halfway up the mountain the pilgrim should begin to see that life is a game that deals more with imperfections than perfections. As human beings, we learn from mistakes on a trial-and-error basis. This does not mean that we should not strive for perfection, but we just should not expect it. The mature Christian finds very little solace from the perfections that he finds within himself. The only perfection he focuses upon is that of the Person of the Lord Jesus Christ. Let us never forget that it is our own imperfection that make us eligible for Christ's salvation. If we could have obtained perfection through our own efforts, then Christ's death would not have been necessary.

It is only when I am aware of the imperfections within myself, that I can see the necessity for moment-by-moment help and guidance from God. The mid-life Christian realizes that one can never reach that level of Christian living from which he can coast into heaven. It is an uphill struggle all the way. If he gets casual about his Christian life, he begins to drift downhill. The Christian can be sure of his eternal destination because of Christ's statement in John 3:16. That gives the Christian a sense of security not available to them who do not believe. But as long as we are in this life, we are going to have to struggle and deal with imperfections.

Each day is a battle, not only in terms of the trials and tribulations from the outside world, but the struggle of the inner battle of the old man and the new. As long as we live as earth creatures, we will have to deal with the old man. The forces that operate in the old man are generated by the power of sin. It is these forces that must be extinguished daily as Paul reminds us. Each day then we must make two claims. First, that the old self died with Christ on the cross, and second that we are alive and sensitive to the call of God through Jesus Christ our Lord. These claims make us aware that the old self had no access to righteousness by any virtues of its own and, as far as God is concerned, is dead. This does not make the individual perfect. It does, however, mean that he can be more completely aware of Christ's perfection, and through that identification, reflect some of the Lord's character of love in his life. The mid-life Christians should not be seasoned actors of a long-running play, whose parts become automatic because of years of repetitious dialogue. Their words and actions should glow and flow with the love that shines clearer and brighter each day. The accessibility to God and His power should be increasingly available. The gaps of indifference, or inattention to His presence, should be less and less.

9
The Person of Christ

For most of us born and raised in so-called Christian countries, the Person of Christ was introduced into our consciousness in the murky realms of childhood. It was then that we first became aware of Christ as the tiny babe in the manger. It was a story that we loved to hear, and it came to us through all the modalities of our senses. We marvelled in the profusion of colors and lights that portrayed that glorious procession; the starlit skies that bathed the rooftops of that tiny mid-eastern town in a mysterious heavenly glow; and the dazzling brilliance of that transcendent star that shown like a tiny sun, lighting the corners of that darkened stall to reveal the glowing face of the blessed virgin and the luminous countenance of the Holy Child. We could not forget the sumptuous gowns of the oriental kings, their golden scepters, and their crowns studded with all of the precious stones known to man. And the music was unforgettable: songs with melodies that never lose their capacity to activate a nostalgic chord somewhere in our hearts and with words of such divine simplicity that they seem oblivious to the higher criticism of sophisticated minds. At no other time in our lives was the fundamental message of Christianity spelled out with such forthright clarity. It was an exciting story to our child-like minds. For our minds, at that time, were inclined to believe anything. So into those repositories went the story with all the other tales of fancy that were part of our psychic worlds at that time. It was a story that was reinforced each year at a time called Christmas. Each year there were, again, the same music, the same story, the same pageantry, but the initial impact of that simplistic story, with its implication of God's involvement in a very special way in each human being's life, began to be diluted. In a curious way, it was the one time of the year when one could give some expression to the spiritual side of life without too much embarrassment. For someone at the fourth hole of a golf match in July, to think about the tiny babe in Bethlehem would either seem like some extreme form of fanaticism or, quite frankly, psychosis.

So as the years passed by, Christmas as an event of *spiritual* significance gradually was filtered out of our minds. It was one of the fairy-tales that seemed so real in those early days of make-believe but lost its substance in the harsh light of reality. And yet, there was something quite different about the Christmas story compared with fairy-tales. For each year that simple story was repeated, if only for a few days. And once in a while, during the brief interval of time, the sound of the bells and the music and the merry atmosphere that surrounded our minds and hearts would overlay one another in a strange juxtaposition that made us sad and joyous at the same time. The collision of thought and feeling did not last very long—no longer than the time to sing a familiar carol, and then we would be swept away with the more exciting aspects of that time of year.

The theme may have been reactivated in those early days of Sunday school when the Bible stories were told with a simplicity that did not attempt to alter the scriptural text, the thought being that children's minds were so extraordinarily gullible that one could tell the story as it was written with no sense of subterfuge. There was yet no reason to demythologize them into psychological parables that would build objective minds that could be useful in the scientific world.

So our first contact with Christ's Person was in those early days of the babe in the manger, and then later in the Sunday school when He was presented as a great moral leader whose platform was love and peace. He, above all, set us a perfect example of living, though in terms of modern-day longevity, He didn't live very long. As a moral code His beatitudes were like advanced calculus compared to the simple mathematics of the Ten Commandments, but as a person, He was always presented as historical, a shadowy figure, somehow linked with God. We had referred to Him as the Son of God in those early days even though we were not quite sure what that meant. It seemed unfair that the good man would be crucified on a cross.

That, of course, brings up the other repeated exposure to the Christ story—the pageant of Easter. Somehow we do not associate the same nostalgic elements with Easter as we do with Christmas. Aside from the hidden baskets of jelly beans and generous supply of chocolate eggs, Easter does not have the same element of giving as Christmas. It is a solemn time, and Good Friday, with all its solemn overtones, was mysterious for most of us as children. In memory, it always seemed like a day when even the sky was overcast. It was also a half-holiday from school or work. Again, the meaning of that holiday became lost in the infiltration of ideas and forces other than Christian. One can recall a sense of pathos in those solemn requiems that were sung by the choirs of many churches at that time. Again, the story of that same mysterious Person who was born in the manger and who by some stroke of injustice ended up on a Roman gibbet. It did not seem fair and most of us could identify with the monstrous injustice of it all, but, as the years passed by, the drama, in terms of what it meant to us as worldlings, became increasingly obscure. In fact, if it were not for the holidays of Christmas and Easter, which seem to be the religious hallmark of nominal Christian nations, the story of the Stranger of Galilee would have taken its place along with *Jack and the Beanstalk* and *The Wizard of Oz*.

In fact, for those of us who became involved with higher education, the concept of the spiritual side of man's nature was swept under the rug as a primitive fantasy, as our minds were encouraged to adapt some scientific model of thought, whether it be Darwinian evolution or Marxian dialetical materialism. To cling to the obsolete notions of Christianity was a betrayal of one's scientific objectivity. The Man of Calvary had some distinctive role in the history of mankind, but man's thinking had not reached that level of sophistication where he could appreciate the concept that there are no absolutes and that everything is in flux and relative.

One wonders in retrospect what these ideas of scientific supremacy did for us except crowd out the archaic thoughts that might indeed have a spiritual component to their nature. Very few of us adopted any identifiable philosophy in our lives, for most of us, living in so-called free societies, became so involved with the materialistic rat race that we had very little time to consider the meaning of our existence. In its briefest form, it could be described as "getting as much pleasure and avoiding as much pain as possible." Something Freud would have described as "primary process thinking."

So as men move into the middle phase of their life experience, they find themselves less and less inclined to consider the spiritual or nonprofitable aspects of their lives and much more inclined to become totally involved with their scramble to the top of the corporate or professional ladder or their entrenchment in the security of a steady job and a fairly predictable future. As life moved on then, there was less and less time and reason for us to think about the spiritual implication of what someone might have done for us 2,000 years ago on an undistinguished hill in an underdeveloped mideastern country. It became increasingly easy for us to accept Christ as an historical figure of questionable significance, if not authenticity, in our very busy lives. As a Person, He had drifted out of our consciousnesses in the turbulence and pressure of those early years of adulthood. It was difficult enough dealing with the people we could see, without becoming involved with some invisible person who had never uttered an audible word within the range of our ears. As a Person, as a real Person, He began to fade in the merry confrontation of Christmas and the dreary encounter of Easter, but now He began to intrude Himself into our lives in the ceremonies of marriages and funerals, which became more frequent in life as we moved towards the top of the mountain. This elusive, yet somehow persistent, Person materialized out of the dialogue of those covenanting voices that proclaimed to one and all that these two people, brought together in holy matrimony, were emulating, in finite form, the eternal and mystical union of Christ and His church. That expression was one of those phrases that drifted quietly over our heads and we took it all in with a minimum of mental exertion in the same way that we absorbed the musical sounds of the church organ.

Perhaps the intrusion of this Person came through more strongly at a funeral. At that most tragic of human events, one was more likely than not to hear during the ceremony the oft-quoted verse, 1 Corinthians 15:55–57, "Oh death, where is thy sting? Oh grave, where is thy victory? The sting of death is sin; and the strength of the sin is the law. But thanks be to God, which giveth us the victory through our Lord Jesus Christ." There's that name again—that Person who has been intruding Himself into our lives since we were tiny tots. Again the significance of that name, no matter what brief comfort it might have given at that sad interlude, is swiftly swallowed up in the acute agony of the parting and further consumed in the powerful forces of forgetfulness—lost to a busy and demanding world. Death is not a theme that the human mind can tolerate for any length of time, nor is Christ the One who allegedly gives us victory over that death. Yet, as we have pointed out elsewhere, death is a reality that begins to take a significant shape in the middle years of life. It is an event that underscores the finitude of man's existence. It is often, in one form or another, the one event that makes a man stop and consider the significance of his life. These deliberations may come to him to take another and closer look at this Stranger of Galilee who has not ceased to follow him in all the steps of his life.

In the years of middle life, the possibility of a spiritual force becomes more and more feasible, depending upon the attitude of the individual toward the patterns in his life at that time. First of all, as we have said repeatedly in this book, he comes into greater confrontation with the concept that all life experiences have optimal limits. To extend beyond the optimal limit, is to court disintegration of that experience. It also becomes increasingly evident that all life events are terminal, that is, they have a beginning and an end. We also become increasingly aware of the fact that all dreams do not necessarily materialize in the form that we first conjured them. Sometimes the dream ends in failure. At other times, it may materialize in ways that far surpass our most extravagant dreams.

Halfway up the mountain we also become aware of the inevitable progression of time. No matter what we do, we are helpless before the inexorable march of time. We also become aware not only of the tyranny of the clock, but the curious distortion of time itself. For as we grow older, twenty years in the past seems but a moment ago, whereas one week in the future can seem like eternity. Then, as we have said elsewhere, these middle years are ones in which we become increasingly aware of a great army of people—beautiful, vital, lovely people who had gone on before us into a realm we rarely take time to consider. These thoughts are disquieting. To some people, they are a nuisance, a form of sickness or negative thinking that they suppress from their busy minds. Their thoughts become concrete. The physical changes of age are challenges to be met with some new hormone or vitamin or some positively charged attitude. These unpleasant intrusions into the painless process of life have no more significance than water in the carburetor of our automobile. The concept that man is in a state of flux, going somewhere, is something that does not occur to many people. Life is now, this is the *now* generation. To this group of people, only the moment has any significance. To think of life as a journey going somewhere, other than the cold rectangle of the grave, is a mild form of delusion.

To these people, the Man of Galilee becomes more of a phantom than He ever was. If they think of Him at all, they see Him only as an increasingly less feasible figure of antiquity that might simply have been a figment of some highly imaginative Jewish mind. Christ then becomes a nonentity to these people. He has no physical substance and, therefore, they can find no room for Him in a purely physical world. These people cling to a physical life that evaporates in their very grasp. Is it any wonder that so many of them become increasingly egocentric and that their lives are characterized by an emotional and material miserliness that makes it very difficult for them to let go of anything or look at anybody but themselves, or to rock the boat of sameness that dominates their lives. To many of these people, the Person of Christ not only becomes increasingly less accessible as life moves on but also becomes tinged with hostility probably because it represents a part of human existence—the spiritual—that they do not want to face. These people are not able to look at reality with the same keenness as one who has acknowledged the spiritual aspect of his life because they see life only the way they want to. They never tire of their rose-tinted glasses.

To another group of people, these uneasy developments of middle life open up a new and exciting area in their thinking. In the face of degenerative changes in the body with their somber message of man's finitude—developments that cause so many of mankind to become involved with defense mechanisms of denial—these people dare to think that life may, indeed, have more significance than the survival of the fittest or the faceless participation in an evolutionary process. They do not see life as an evolutionary process that may, at some unpredictable point in time, produce a superman who will not get old or tired or fat or be subject to any of the other unpleasant things that plague us poor mortals, who find ourselves stuck at a lower echelon of the evolutionary scale. These people resist the regressive pull of egocentricity that forces their attention in upon themselves and make the tiny sphere of existence they occupy the only significant perspective in the universe. They are not afraid to see themselves in the infinitesimal dimension in which they must appear to someone viewing them from some distant planet. The mid-life shock of the finitude of man makes people more accessible to the spiritual side of their natures. To those who respond to this spiritual stimulus, it is a transcendent experience. The one-way pull of material reality loses its attractive force. The Stranger of Galilee becomes more accessible and, at some point in time, may burst into their lives like an explosion of sunshine leading them into a way of life they never dreamed of before. The distant sound of carols awaken something more than a nostalgic dream of childhood. They introduce, in a very remarkable way, a Person who becomes more real than oneself. The Bible is no longer a book that fits into a category of fiction that includes *Grimm's Fairytales* and *Aesop's Fables*. It becomes what Francis Schaeffer describes as God's "propositional, verbalized communication to men that is true about God, true about history, and true about the cosmos." God speaks not in a voice measured by decibels, but by the silent messages of His Word, the Bible. It is from these words that the Person of Christ begins to emerge in a way that is far more compelling than the physical witnessing of His own historical life. We begin to see the significance of the cross as something more than a symbol of one of the larger religions of the world. We see it as the historical manifestation of a love that far exceeds the understanding of man, a love that compelled the Apostle Paul to declare in Romans 8:38, 39, "For I am persuaded, that neither death, nor life, nor angels, nor principalities, nor powers, nor things present, nor things to come, Nor height, nor depth, nor any other creature, shall be able to separate us from the love of God, which is in Christ Jesus our Lord." That is the kind of love that exceeds all the concepts of love that man has ever imagined. For this is a unilateral relationship, one that never gives up and one that is never restricted by the rejection or acceptance of the human person.

In quiet retrospect, the responsive person can see how Christ never gave up in His quest for the person's love at any moment in that person's life. He sadly reflects how many times he callously closed the door in the Lord's face because Christ did not seem to be relevant in his life situation at that time.

So the Person of Christ grows more real, not by the clustering of molecules into some physical form, nor the advent of a glowing presence, nor a resonant voice out of the darkness of the night. The Person of Christ becomes substantiated in the life of the Christian, first of all, by the action of the Holy Spirit that exploits every nuance of human experience to reveal that Christ did something very special for every one of us, that the cross is more than a universal symbol of sacrifice or self-denial. It is the door to a new way of life, not by some clever alteration of psychic perspective, but by a love relationship with another Person that exceeds all of the love relationships that we may have had with human beings.

So, first as humans, we are aware of this extraordinary love. The Person at first remote, comes closer and closer into focus as the rays of that love begin to penetrate our beings. Our hearts are directed to communicate with Him in prayer, prayers that at first may be tentative babblings from tongues not yet able to participate in the one-way communication, as it seems from the human perspective. As we come to rely more and more upon the Holy Spirit, we begin to experience a quiet power of direction that causes our hearts and tongues to praise God in ways that far surpass our human intellects. The Christian gradually becomes aware of the leading of the Holy Spirit, that mysterious, but very real, force that operates in the life of every Christian. It confirms,

yet again, the promise of the Lord that He would never leave us
without a Comforter. The Comforter produces within the Christian a new kind of awareness. We become very clearly aware of
God's hand in every step of our earthly pathway.

The most precise form of communication about the Person of
Christ comes to us through the Bible, for it is in the pages of
God's Word that the Person of Christ comes to us in a very real
way, because the Bible is more than a treasury of moral and
ethical statements. It is the revelation to all mankind of the Person of the Lord Jesus Christ. As the Christian studies that Word
each day, the Lord as a Person becomes more real. The presence
of the Lord in the Christian's life is as real as the awareness of his
own body. The loneliness that is part of the egocentric design of
human life is replaced by the constant communication with the
Person of his new friend and companion.

So the threatening developments of mid-life do not drive the
new Christian into a regressive retreat of denial. He is not afraid
to confront life as it is. The honesty of this new way of life is very
refreshing to him. It is like being in the fresh mountain air after
years in the polluted climes of the city. The disintegration of his
physical being does not cause him to cower in the corner. He
accepts all these changes as part of God's wonderful plan for him.
The specter of death is no threat to him. Death is not the end, it is
the beginning of a new kind of relationship with his precious
Lord. No longer is there any need to study Scripture for some
extra morsel of revelation for he has a full, unimpaired view of his
Saviour's face. As the new Christian looks up the mountain to
higher elevations, which become increasingly precipitous as
human experiences but more comforting in the full maturity of
Christian life, he feels no fear, but a warm sense of getting closer
and closer to his blessed goal.

There are some people who met the real Christ in the early days
of their lives—people whose contact with Him goes back many,
many years. When these privileged people reach mid-life, the
Person of Christ should be very real to them. They should know

Him as the secret sharer of every moment of their lives. Their lives should now begin to reflect Christ in all of its movements. The same wisdom that directed His life, should direct theirs.

We think of His function as Creator "For by Him were all things created, that are in heaven, and that are in earth, visible and invisible." (*See* Colossians 1:16.) How easy it is for us to overlook His function as Creator of everything, to forget that every created thing is a reflection of His image. Not only did He create everything, but by His power all things that are created are held together. The totality of that concept is really too great for the human mind to comprehend, but we can understand it to the degree that we are aware that all created things are a further reflection of Him. In our petty busyness we may overlook that aspect of His person. But halfway up the mountain, the Christian should be more and more aware of Christ's creative capacity in all areas of life. As we view every creative thing, we, in a sense, view Him. As we listen to Beethoven's Third Symphony we may appreciate the sheer beauty of the music, but, in appreciation of that music, we may forget the fact that the beauty of that music is a reflection of the One who created the music, not Ludwig von Beethoven, for he was simply the channel through which that talent came. Beethoven's musical genius was a gift. The Giver and the Creator of that gift was the Lord Jesus Christ. As we move into the years of maturity, we begin to see more clearly that all talents, no matter where they may appear, are gifts from God. The person who receives the talent is responsible for the fulfillment of that talent. Many gifted people never allow their talents to develop. This is a tragedy. What is also puzzling, from a human point of view, is that God seems to be without discrimination in His distribution of gifts. From the human perspective, it would seem fairer that talent should go to the people who are going to prove to be worthy, but the Lord, who is free of human weaknesses and prejudices, distributes gifts in a completely unprejudiced way. The worst kind of scoundrel may have a very special gift that God has not seen fit to begrudge him. In the very distribution of that talent, we see the beautiful quality of God's unmerited grace.

The ultimate example of that grace is God's gift of His own Son for a rebellious and callous humanity. The awareness of this quality in God's nature makes us less intimidated by what would seem, from the perspective of this world, as unfairness. Why shouldn't the good people always win? What we begin to see is that maybe they do, but their victory is not in the soon-to-be-forgotten victories of this world but in the heavenly triumph that reverberates to the far reaches of the universe. We begin to see that God gave such-and-such a person a particular talent because that was the only possible way that that person could be reached for God. God's method of reaching another person may not be through the avenues of earthly accomplishment but through the humility that comes with defeat.

What seems to emerge is a priority system that is often paradoxical in terms of what the world thinks is important. It is as though the Christian, through his identification with Christ, begins to sense that some of his basic instincts are changing. The one ingredient that seems to be the prime mover is love. Now as we have said elsewhere, love is a concept that the world also embraces, but, as we have also indicated, the world's love is reciprocal. Its integrity is based upon the reaction of not only the one who loves, but also the one who is being loved. One of the reasons that the love of this world is so tenuous is because it is based upon the variable factor of reciprocation. If the love is not mutual, it begins to degenerate. If there is one thing that the mid-life Christian is aware of, it is the unilateral aspect of God's love. Time and time again we fail Christ in our lives. The only thing He asks to prove our love is obedience. "If ye love me, keep my commandments." (John 14:15.) Sounds easy, but, in minds and bodies that are never totally free from the influences of sin, that obedience, at times, becomes very difficult. In mid-life the Christian should begin to be aware of the beauty of that obedience. It is a refining process that makes him more synchronous with his Lord. Obedience is the proof of our love.

As we reflect upon His life, we see that it was characterized by obedience, not an obedience that underscored the perfection of His life, but an obedience of such beauty that it reflected His deep love for God the Father. There is a certain security in the act of obedience that is difficult to define. It involves trust, subordination of the ego, self-sacrifice, and a willingness to endure hardship and even pain. Now when love is the motivating force behind such obedience, it produces within the obedient person a sense of security that is difficult to duplicate. The Lord has given us in His life an example of obedience that reflects His great love for the Father. What greater act of obedience could there be than the cross itself? Listen to Christ in the garden, in Matthew 26:39, ". . . O my Father, if it be possible, let this cup pass from me: nevertheless not as I will, but as thou wilt."

The act of obedience which He was about to undergo, was not a pleasant task. It was an act of total obedience by a Son who had obeyed every facet of His Father's will. For Christ's was a life that only knew the experience of complete harmony with the Father whom He loved. Now He was asked to take upon Himself the sin burden of the whole world. The One who was repulsed by any suggestion of sin was to become saturated with the sin of rebellious mankind. He obeyed not only because it was His Father's will, but also because He loved the world. His death upon the cross was the ultimate expression of obedience and love.

The mid-life Christian should become increasingly aware of that characteristic of obedience which was such an important part of the Saviour's life. That same mixture of love and obedience should begin to show itself in the life of the mature Christian, not only as a testimony to the external world of the linkage of that person with God the Father, but, more important, as it manifests itself as an expression of love in the inner world of the Christian.

We cannot overlook the Lord's role as peacemaker. It was a

peace that He provided and that He promised every believer. "Peace I leave with you, my peace I give unto you: not as the world giveth, give I unto you." (John 14:27.) The peace that He gave to us was not the kind that nations agree to—peace that is dependent upon conditions set forth on a piece of paper. His peace is not determined by a series of conditions. There is only one condition—that we accept it. His peace is a gift. It is a peace that transcends every human condition. It is not a peace that shields us from all the things that happened to the rest of mankind. It is a peace that allows us to see and experience all of the vicissitudes of life with an inner equanimity and quietness that this world can never know. It is indeed the peace that passes human understanding. It is a peace that flourishes in the midst of the turmoil of this world, whether it be famine, war, poverty, or death.

One of the most important things that begins to come through, in the life of the person who has known the Lord for any length of time, is the importance of learning to abide in Him. To abide, Webster says, means to "stand fast or to go on being." What this seems to suggest is that abiding is a very active process. It is not reaching a goal and then resting on one's laurels. It means to stand firm, or never retreat, with what we have, and to go on in the process of our growth as Christians. We as branches of the vine, Christ, must hold fast to that vine, for it is through that vine that life itself comes with all of the ingredients that make that life continue.

What should be coming through to the Christian in mid-life is the reality of Jesus Christ as a Person. I think that is one reason why we see so many contradictory Christians—people who say and apparently believe one thing, but whose life bears very little evidence of their beliefs. Christ is not very real to them in the nitty-gritty of day-to-day life. It is as though they have made no place for Him in the compartment of their day-to-day living.

This is such an easy thing *not* to do. It is the very problem the

Lord was referring to when He spoke to His disciples in the Passover chamber before His crucifixion. When Philip indicated that the only acceptable proof of the Lord's oneness with the Father would be if the Lord could demonstrate the Father in a physical way to them. The Lord looked at him and made what, to me, is one of the saddest statements in all of the Bible. "Jesus saith unto him, Have I been so long time with you, and yet hast thou not known me, Philip?" (John 14:9.) I often wonder if the Lord could not be saying the same thing to a lot of Christians, who have been acquainted with Him since childhood but whc have never really gotten to know Him. At mid-life they know all of the words that Christians use, they know the numbers of the hymns and can quote verbatim long passages of Scripture, but the fact of the matter is, they do not seem to *know* Him. For to know Him is to reflect Him in all minutia of life, to be aware of His presence at all times—not just in the times of crisis or sickness, or death. We hear a great deal about the word *share* these days. Basically it pertains to sharing experiences with other human beings. As important as that concept may be in the lives of human beings, it is nowhere near as important as meaningful sharing of one's life with the Lord Jesus Christ. It is that sense of sharing that brings the reality of Christ into sharper focus in the individual's life. I wonder how many of us miss Him when He does not seem to be there? The truth of the matter is, we know He is always there, as His very last words indicate, ". . . and, lo, I am with you alway, even unto the end of the world." (Matthew 28:20.) One does not know exactly how long Philip was with the Lord, but of one thing we can be sure: it was a fraction of the time that most mid-life Christians have had with Him. It is in this phase of their existence that the Lord's presence should be permeating every aspect of their lives.

Yes, I know that some people will say that Philip knew Him for only a few years, but he knew Him in a very special way. He actually saw Him, heard His voice, and touched His hand. It is that physical dimension that makes the difference, we think, but is that not the same kind of thinking that Philip himself was involved with? Lord, show us some physical evidence of God's presence and it will suffice us. Had Philip forgotten Lazarus? Had he not witnessed the Lord's walking on the sea? the healing of the man who was blind from his birth? How could there possibly be any need for more proof?

Physical proof of God, physical contact with Him can never be realized in our finite existence. No one ever believed God through some mathematical proof. The most intimate of physical contact comes to an end and sets up another need for contact.

In a curious way, our relationship with Christ as twentieth-century beings is much more intimate than it ever could have been if we had related to Him when He was on the earth as a physical presence. For, being human, He would be subject to all of the principles that operate in our physical world. When he went out of our sight, we could no longer see Him. When His voice was beyond the range of our ears, we could no longer hear Him. Now we have access to Him, as the indwelling Christ, no matter where we go. He can never go beyond our vision, or our ears, or our touch, for His promise is a constant fellowship that will never be nullified. With the accessibility of that kind of relationship, how sad, then, that we can be with Him so long and yet not know Him.

How beautiful it is halfway up the mountain for those who not only believe Him, but also know Him. Down below we can see our past life with some patches of bright green where the sun shines through and other areas where there appear to be dark valleys. Already the mists begin to gather around us, at first like slender threads. As we look upward, we begin to be especially aware of the peak. It is not that at this perspective we feel particularly heavenly, but now we can begin to enjoy life with a depth and richness never available before. We can face directly certain aspects of life that we were afraid to deal with before—life's brevity, our smallness as individuals in an enormous universe, the ceaseless flow of time, the inevitability of weather, and death itself. Our ability to assimilate these things and not to shy away from them fills us with a sense of responsibility for others along the side of this rugged mountain. It makes us sensitive to their needs. It can cause us to include them in our prayers and to reach out to them in every way possible. It makes us aware of how absolutely necessary it is for us to depend upon God for everything in our lives. It allows us to reach an intimacy with Him that combines worship and action in a way that cannot be exceeded in any other part of our lives. We are halfway up the mountain, but with knowledge of God's love and dependence upon Him, we can say with Paul, "I press toward the mark for the prize of the high calling of God in Christ Jesus" (Philippians 3:14).